Copyright © 2024 by Ashton Bro,

No part of this publication may be reproduced,
distributed, or transmitted in any form or by any means,
including photocopying, recording, or other electronic
or mechanical methods, without the prior written
permission of the publisher.

"Scripture quotations are from the ESV® Bible (The
Holy Bible, English Standard Version®), © 2001 by
Crossway, a publishing ministry of Good News
Publishers. Used by permission. All rights reserved."

TMM PUBLISHING

P.O. Box 5861

Deltona FL 32724

www.TMMPublishing.com

ISBN: 979-8-9914060-9-3

Big Yellow HOUSE

God's Goodness Revealed: Growing Through
Hardship in Marriage and Health while on
the Path to Adoption

Ashton Draper

Dedication

To Zyan, Nyla, Bismark, and Liam: I pray that you come to know the Lord and share your unique adoption stories with the world. Love, Mama

Acknowledgments

I would like to show my gratitude to all those who made this book possible.

First and foremost, my Lord and Savior Jesus Christ. It may sound cliché, but this story is His. He is the Author and the One who makes all things work together for our good.

My biggest shout-out is to my husband, Spencer: thank you for encouraging me to step into this and be vulnerable in my writing... I appreciate your support and help in putting this book together. Thank you for your unwavering commitment to me through the challenges we have faced. You really are the better half.

I am eternally grateful for our kids. Zyan, Nyla, and Liam: thank you for embracing the adoption and being the best siblings throughout the process.

You are resilient, loving, and brave. Bismark: Thank you for teaching me a new kind of love. All four of you bring such joy and blessing to my life.

To our parents and siblings: they say it takes a village to raise children, and this part of that village holds a special place in my heart. Thank you simply isn't enough.

To all of our family and friends: thank you for always being there for my family when we needed you. We truly have the best village.

To the Church: You all came together locally and globally, across denominations and differences, to help make our story a reality. Thank you.

To all the people who supported us financially: Our adoption would not have been possible without you. Thank you for playing an integral role in bringing Bismark home.

I am also extremely grateful for our counselor: Thank you for continually challenging us to live lives that glorify the Lord and pointing us back to Jesus. You have truly changed my perspective.

Finally, a huge thank you to my readers and those who encouraged me to write a book—your enthusiasm led me here, and I am so thankful to share more of our story with you.

Endorsements

By writing this book, Ashton is, yet again, a beautiful example of what it means to selflessly take the leap of faith into what God calls us to do. To say that she has had her fair share of ups and downs would be a considerable understatement. As we read, she lovingly takes us through a beautiful and inspirational journey of battling health issues, the trials of overseas adoption, navigating the struggles of marriage, and spiritual warfare. A devout Christian with unwavering faith, a loving and patient mother, and one of my favorite people in the entire world, Ashton is living proof that all things are possible when you keep your eyes on Jesus!

-Jayden Conley, Ashton's oldest brother

When I sit down to read this book, it's as if I am sitting across from the Drapers over a cup of coffee, eagerly listening to each intricate part of their journey. As I read the words on the pages, I cannot help but engage my own emotions as it challenges my heart and soul to depend on Jesus in my own life. The heart-wrenching, raw, and beautiful story of their journey is out for all to see. They've faced deep valleys, moments of health crises, a marriage on the brink, and the emotional rollercoaster of adoption—times when it felt like Satan was relentlessly trying to derail the future God had promised them. But God held them together through every tear, prayer, and moment they felt like giving up. On the other side of their pain, they've found unimaginable blessings and a depth of love and growth they never expected. This is a story of relentless faith, enduring hope, and the powerful beauty of God's redemption. As you interact with their story, be sure to examine your own life… when you do that, you cannot walk away from these pages and not be transformed!

-Logan Conley, Ashton's older brother

Table of Contents

Preface

As people encouraged me to write a book on our international adoption journey, I really considered if it was something I was capable of doing. English was never my strongest subject, and I simply never thought of myself as a writer. I knew that if I was going to write a book, the story had to include the surrounding circumstances and life that happened simultaneously with the adoption. No journey happens within a vacuum, and in that same light, I have learned that anything that happens in the physical has a spiritual component behind it. Nothing is neutral. As we started our adoption journey, my health and our marriage took a journey of their own (or so we thought they were separate journeys).

If there is one thing I have learned throughout the past several years, it is that Satan is a very real enemy. Anything that happens in the physical is also a spiritual battle for the soul. It wasn't until recently that I thoroughly learned and understood this concept and how it has played out in my life. You see, Satan is like a prowling lion (1 Peter 5:8). Just like a lion studies its prey before attacking, Satan knows all the right tactics, so when he does attack, he seemingly has a leg up on the competition. I say seemingly because, spoiler alert, Jesus ultimately claims victory. We, as Christians, can allow God to use Satan's attacks to help us become more like Jesus if we are aware of the battle taking place for our souls. The right perspective changes everything. I didn't (and still don't) always have the right perspective. I am still growing in this and trying not to lose sight of the battle and lesson in the middle of my life's hard moments.

When starting to venture to write this book, I heard the enemy whisper, "You can't write about your medical journey because you haven't found physical healing," and "you can't write about marital healing when you are still in marriage counseling." But then I heard the Lord whisper, "You aren't writing about finding physical healing or the perfect marriage. You are writing about finding ME in the midst of your challenging circumstances." If you are experiencing challenges, struggling to persevere, losing hope in a situation, or simply want to be encouraged to keep fighting the good fight for the Lord, this book is for you. In light of all of this, please join me on the multi-faceted, physical, and spiritual journey of international adoption, chronic illness, and marriage.

CHAPTER 1

A Little Girl's Heart

What is it for you…that gentle nudging or, perhaps, violent pulling at your heart? What makes your heart leap for joy or churn with anxious anticipation at simply the mention of it? Maybe you have a passion, something you love or desire, that is unexplored. Maybe it is an unchartered territory that terrifies you at the thought of jumping into. Maybe a price tag flashes in your mind leaving you crippled at the seeming impossibility of the dream. Maybe the journey has too many unknowns that aren't worth discovering for yourself. Maybe the risk is too great. Maybe your family requires too much from you, or maybe you feel insignificant and inadequate in pursuing your passion. Maybe people speak negativity into existence surrounding your desires. Or maybe, just maybe, there is a small seed of doubt in your mind that says you can't pursue or achieve your dream, no matter how small or grandiose. Can I just say something? I wrestled with many of these same feelings as well.

It would be simple to say that this journey started over five years ago when my husband, Spencer, and I first signed a contract with an adoption agency to begin our international adoption. However, the reality is that the story began decades ago. It began in a little girl's heart...my heart. I can't define the moment that I knew I wanted to adopt. I can only recall a tug in my heart towards adoption as a young girl and then reoccurring as the years went by. I may not be able to define the timing of everything as it pertains to my desire to adopt, but I am able to say that Africa has always been in my heart. For whatever reason, I knew the Lord was directing my path to Africa.

Knowing my heart's desire to adopt, I had to be upfront with Spencer when we started dating. Thankfully, he was open to adoption in the future despite neither of us knowing what that would look like. God withholding the details of what it would look like is an example of His grace. Had we known what it would entail or the opposition we would face, we may not have embarked on the journey to begin with. I say this to show you that I am much like you, and Spencer and I are much like many other married couples. We are not extraordinary people, but rather ordinary people, allowing God to do extraordinary things through us. As He leads us, we are being shaped and molded into His image as we go. Our adoption journey (and life surrounding it) has been full of many challenging circumstances that we never anticipated. Extremely challenging. We are not special for enduring it. We are just leaning into Jesus to get us through it. And can I be honest for a moment? We spent time during the journey NOT leaning into Jesus and just trying to get through it on our own, failing miserably. I think that's reality. Our pursuit of holiness is not linear. We all fall down and make mistakes along the way. It is okay to be honest in our failures and acknowledge that Jesus was carrying us and pursuing us even when we weren't pursuing Him.

The Bible speaks to the idea of adoption in regard to how Christians should treat orphans. James 1:27 says, "Religion that is pure and undefiled before God the Father is this: to visit orphans and widows in their affliction, and to keep oneself unstained from the world." Does that mean I believe EVERY Christian should adopt? Not necessarily. I think an argument could be made one way or the other. However, I do think adoption can be a very powerful display of who Jesus is and His heart for the outcast. James 1:27 points us in the direction of taking care of the marginalized in society.

Adoption is often romanticized, and I believe I fell into the trap of viewing it that way. Don't get me wrong, adoption is beautiful. However, adoption is also hard and comes at a cost. It's messy and hard because its necessity is a result of sin. One of my favorite quotes concerning the "costliness" of adoption says, "My friends, adoption is redemption. It's costly, exhausting, expensive, and outrageous. Buying back lives costs so much. When God set out to redeem us, it killed Him." (Derek Loux, late adoptive parent)

God never intended for adoption to be a system put into place for a child to have parents. He also never designed us to need to be adopted through His son, but He did it anyway. He made a way for us and had a perfect plan of redemption when we messed it all up. In the book of Genesis, we see that God created man in His image. God and man were in perfect relationship with one another. When sin entered the picture, things changed. It caused an eternal separation from God, which created a need for us to find a way back to the Father. Thankfully, God paved the way for us through His Son. Just like the orphans who receive parents, the Bible tells us that Christians are also adopted, which is why pursuing adoption is a beautiful picture of the gospel. Ephesians 1:5 says, "he predestined us for adoption to himself as sons through Jesus Christ, according to the purpose of his will." Because Jesus Christ died for our sins, when we choose to follow Him, we become sons of His father, God himself. We also become co-heirs with Jesus. Romans 8:15-17 says, "For you did not receive the spirit of slavery to fall back into fear, but you have received the Spirit of adoption as sons, by whom we cry, 'Abba! Father!' The spirit Himself bears witness with our spirit that we are children of God, and if children, then heirs – heirs of God and fellow heirs with Christ, provided we suffer with him in order that we may also be glorified with him." Not only are we children adopted by God, but we are also like brothers and sisters to Christ.

Because adoption has the potential to paint a beautiful picture of redemption and likens us to the orphan in need of a heavenly Father, we have an Enemy who doesn't want God to be glorified through the act of adoption. 2 Corinthians 10:3-5 says, "For though we walk in the flesh, we are not waging war according to the flesh. For the weapons of our warfare are not of the flesh but have divine power to destroy strongholds. We destroy arguments and every lofty opinion raised against the knowledge of God, and take every thought captive to obey Christ." It is important to be aware of the war that we do fight, a spiritual war in which Satan is crafty, but the power of God in us is so much greater.

When we follow the biblical passions God puts in our hearts, we have to be prepared for battle, which I was not when the Lord laid adoption on mine. Ephesians 6:11-13 says, "Put on the whole armor of God, that you may be able to stand against the schemes of the devil. For we do not wrestle against flesh and blood, but against the rulers, against the authorities, against the cosmic powers over this present darkness, against the spiritual forces of evil in the heavenly places. Therefore take up the whole armor of God, that you may be able to withstand in the evil day, and having done all, to stand firm." We prepare for the battle by putting on the armor of God and fighting in a way contrary to how the world fights. The armor of God helps us stand firm in our faith when adversity hits. This is something I really learned and have become increasingly aware of as we have pursued and stepped into what God had for us. Saying yes to the pursuit of adoption was an avenue in which God shaped both Spencer and me as we took one step at a time into the good, bad, and ugly of the journey.

So, for me, the nagging and tugging was adoption. But the reality is God has also given you a passion and gift for which you were specifically created. In fact, you are called to something that only you were made to fulfill. Romans 12:6 says, "Having gifts that differ according to the grace given to us, let us use them..." In Ephesians 2:10, we see that "We are his workmanship, created in Christ Jesus for good works, which God prepared beforehand, that we should walk in them." God had a purpose for you from the beginning. If you allow any or all of those stumbling blocks mentioned at the beginning of this chapter to keep you exactly where you are, you will miss out on witnessing the

Lord work miracles through your gifts and on the blessing waiting on the other side.

If you call yourself a follower of Jesus, you have the light of Jesus inside of you that is meant to shine in the darkness. John 1:5 says, "The light shines in the darkness, and the darkness has not overcome it." Your gift or passion may call you into dark places, which is exactly where the light of Jesus shines the brightest. Step into the gift and passion you were given and allow your light to shine in dark places, growing and becoming more like Jesus in the process. I have prayed over this book that those who pick it up would step into their gifts and passions. My desire is that waves of Jesus-followers would reach the dark places, knowing a spiritual battle is taking place but trusting that Jesus will overcome and be glorified. Friends, put on the whole armor of God every single day as you seek to shine your light and knowingly step into battle "…that you may be able to stand against the schemes of the devil." (Ephesians 6:12) It was because of my belief in the gift and passion for

12

adoption laid on my heart by the Giver that I did not give up when the Enemy tried to thwart the plans and path we began. My prayer is that you will be encouraged by our story and that our story allows you to be honest about yours.

Challenge/Question for Thought: What are your passions? What holds you back from pursuing them? If you are pursuing them, how can you use them to glorify God, who is the giver of your gifts?

CHAPTER 2

Ghana Chose Us

Waiting for the "right" time to adopt is tricky. There is no magic in making that decision. There is no right time for you to have enough money. There is no way of predicting how long the process will take. And there is certainly no guarantee that the process will go smoothly. That being said, in the fall of 2018, Spencer and I began exploring the idea of adoption. At the time, we had been married for five years, had Zyan (our two-year-old daughter) and Nyla (our months-old baby), and plans to have another kid (or kiddos) in the future. I spent hours searching online, exploring different adoption agencies and country programs, and then calling to gather more information. I kept notes on which agencies and countries would be the best fit for our family. Sadly, we had heard many horror stories of people who were scammed by seemingly legitimate adoption agencies, so doing my best to find a great agency was of utmost importance.

After many conversations, we settled on the reality that "now" wasn't a good time to adopt. Unfortunately, each country had very specific requirements, and we didn't meet them. Some countries required a long stay in-country of six months or more, which didn't seem feasible with work schedules and leaving life at home for so long. Other countries required children to be adopted in birth order, which was not something we could agree to since we still wanted to grow our biological family. Other countries required couples to have been married longer than we were at the time or that both Spencer and I had to be a certain age, which we were not. Some countries required fewer biological children than we had or were planning to have. Other countries mainly adopted out older children, which did not match our criteria. So, we put the adoption on hold, trusting that the door for adoption would open when the Lord deemed it best.

Fast forward to the beginning of 2019. I hadn't done more research or leaned into adoption since the fall and hadn't even given it much more thought. However, because I had done so much research, Google knew exactly what information to share with the appropriate organizations. When people ask why we chose Ghana, we say, "We didn't; Ghana chose us!" Let me tell you why. We received a call from an adoption agency out of North Carolina informing us that Ghana, Africa had just opened up its doors to international adoption once again. It isn't uncommon for countries to open and close their doors to adoption for a variety of reasons. Adoptions had taken place in Ghana previously, but the program for international adoption had been shut down for some time. Ghana underwent the requirements to become a Hague Convention country, allowing international adoptions to begin again. Becoming a Hague Convention country meant that they went through the legalities to become a country whose goal is to ensure that adoptions are safe and in the best interest of the child.

The agency informed us of the different requirements to adopt from Ghana. The program only required families to stay in the country for one month, and there were options to adopt younger children. We met the marriage and biological children requirements. We informed the agency of our desire to continue to grow our biological family to make sure that wouldn't be an issue. We kept the conversation open, asked a lot of questions, and made sure that this was the direction we wanted to take. To add to all of the unknowns of adoption, because the country had recently re-opened its doors, we would be joining the pilot program if we chose to move forward. Joining a pilot program basically means those first families in the program are guinea pigs. It would be nearly impossible to predict how the process would go because everything from Ghana's side of things was brand new, meeting new requirements that they never had before. After many conversations and considerations, in February 2019, we signed the contract to begin the adoption process!

Starting the adoption process meant quite a bit of work for me. Because I worked part-time and stayed home taking care of the kids, I had more time to commit to filling out paperwork, planning fundraisers, preparing the home for a home study, etc. I set out to do just that. I filled out oodles of paperwork, bought necessary items for our home to meet the home study requirements, and began planning our first fundraiser. When we signed the contract with our agency, we also had to agree to the financial implications and fees associated with the adoption. Taking on an international adoption doesn't make sense at the surface level. The financial implications are astronomical. The average family cannot realistically afford such an undertaking. And trust me, we are only average. I would argue that we were actually less than average, with me only working part-time in addition to Spencer's hourly job. Throwing fundraisers and applying for grants were critical parts of the process for us. We signed the contract trusting that the Lord would provide for every financial need since He called us into this adoption.

I am thankful that we didn't have the money to pay for the adoption on our own. Because we had to rely on the Lord to provide, we got to know Him as the Provider. We sing songs and acknowledge with our lips that the Lord is our provider, but until we are in a position in which we need to be provided for, we don't have personal knowledge of how the Lord is our Provider. If I were to show you the numbers for the cost of the adoption, you would likely shudder at the price and wonder why it is so expensive. You would probably feel similar to us in that we didn't have the financial means to follow such a call on our lives. We certainly didn't know where the money would come from. But, if I were to tell you that the Lord provided every penny necessary (and He did!), I hope that the numbers would encourage you because of how big of a God we really serve. We had to step out in faith and watch the Lord work. Faith doesn't make sense to our mortal minds. The faith muscle is built when we step out in obedience, and then the Lord shows up. We had the funds come in through many grants and faithful friends and family. The Church did what it was called to do when it answered the call to help us financially. Because of our supporters, I am even more encouraged and inspired to support and pour into others taking on Godly endeavors to further the kingdom.

I have to wonder, how often are we in a situation in which, without God's intervention, things will fail? Like, truly? Do we ever position ourselves in a way in which we NEED God to show up because it is impossible otherwise? How often do we say "yes" to things that don't add up because we don't have the means? I would venture to say almost never. I know I am guilty of this. We like to sit with comfortable bank accounts, savings in the case of emergencies, and 401ks to be comfortable in retirement. These things are not inherently bad. In fact, the Bible has a lot to say about wisdom, and I think it can be wise to save money. However, the thought of dipping into any of these areas of financial protection (or not having them in the first place) paralyzes us in fear that we won't have the money when we really need it instead of trusting that the Lord will provide it. Luke 12:24 says, "Consider the ravens: they neither sow nor reap, they have neither storehouse nor barn, and yet God feeds them. Of how much more value are you than the birds!" We can rest assured that the Lord will provide for our daily needs. We can see how God does just that when we read about the Israelites going from Egypt to the Promised Land. God instructs them to gather just enough manna every day to be enough for THAT day. God provided their daily bread just like He provides ours. We are living proof that if God places a calling upon your life, He will sustain you and provide for that calling as you live out it.

When we agreed to the fee schedule from our agency that required the Lord to show up, we had no idea the additional fees and expenses that would present themselves in our future as we waited to

21

finalize the adoption. As you are well aware, the COVID pandemic took place 2020, just one year after signing our contract. It may seem as if that would be unrelated to our adoption, but it had huge financial implications. COVID-19 created a situation in which the adoption process stalled significantly only one year into the process. There were no social workers going out in the fields in Ghana to do the necessary paperwork to determine whether a child was adoptable or not. This likely stalled the adoption by one and a half to two years. While this may only seem like a timing issue, it is also a financial issue. Our international home study was only valid for 15 months. We had an initial home study done in 2019 when we began the adoption and ended up having to update the home study three times before we went to Ghana. When you update a home study, you also have to update fingerprinting and medical exams, all of which cost time and money. We also had to sign and pay for an annual contract with our agency to stay in the program with them.

The timing of COVID-19 in the middle of our journey created more space for Satan to attack our family. In the same breath, I would say that it also created more space for God to work in ways that only He can and write our story for us. I never want to acknowledge Satan without also acknowledging the God we serve. While Satan may be the ruler of this world (John 16:11), God has the final say. Nothing happens without God allowing it to. So, it is important that we acknowledge the spiritual element taking place in our lives and engage in the battle. We are promised that the battle will come, and we must fight as to fight for the Lord. All of that to say that while in the waiting, I underwent a series of medical complexities that rocked our world both physically, mentally, relationally, emotionally, financially, and spiritually, which I will delve into next.

Challenge/Question for Thought: What is God calling you to that you have not answered because you don't have the means to follow through with it?

23

Do you TRULY trust that the Lord will provide for your every need, even when it seems impossible?

CHAPTER 3

Medical Complexities

In the summer of 2019, we got pregnant with our third child, and in February 2020, I gave birth to Liam. Prior to his birth, I had three great pregnancies as well as two amazing delivery stories. Immediately following Liam's birth, I knew something was wrong. There was a lot of quiet talk between the doctors and nurses, but I was wrapped up in love for my newborn baby. When they called in an OB doctor, things changed rather quickly. My placenta did not come out completely, and I began hemorrhaging. Immediately, I signed the paperwork for surgery and agreed to a hysterectomy if deemed necessary during surgery. I remember the feeling of blood loss, the cold and sterile environment of the operating room, and the anesthesiologist announcing I had to be put under because I couldn't even sit up to receive a spinal block. It was all so clear and yet all so cloudy. I remember my inability to really think or quickly process anything. I remember passing out as I was forced to lie down before surgery. I had a life-saving surgery that evening and several blood transfusions in the following days. It was certainly a birth that we had not anticipated, but we are so thankful the Lord kept me safe.

One month later, I had another surgery related to my initial post-partum complications. This was completely unexpected and a mystery to the doctors who cared for me. Surgery number two. Thankfully, recovery from this second surgery went well. Simultaneously, the COVID-19 pandemic entered the picture. In many ways, I loved having time alone to snuggle Liam as much as I could since we were uncertain if more babies would be in our future. But as it did for many, COVID-19 invoked a level of fear with all of the unknowns.

As a result of COVID, my job became a remote job, and I moved into my basement for work a few months post-surgery. In the summer of 2020, I started to feel "off" and just unwell more often than I ever had before. I distinctly remember a week in July in which I began to wonder what may be wrong, but I never pursued finding an answer. In September 2020, I contracted a minor case of COVID-19 that I healed from quickly. I dealt with the loss of taste and smell and fatigue. Outside of that, my body handled it very well.

Shortly following that illness, I had still been feeling unwell with generalized abdominal pain. I decided to seek treatment at a walk-in clinic when the ill feeling and pain didn't go away. One thing led to another, and we discovered I had kidney stones. They were not stuck, so it wasn't urgent. However, they were likely moving and causing discomfort. Due to their size, it wasn't possible for them to pass on their own when the time would come. In October 2020, I had a lithotripsy to break up the kidney stones so that I could pass them. Surgery number three. Two days later, the broken-apart pieces all got stuck, so I went in for another procedure to place a stent for the kidney stones to pass. Surgery number four.

Time went on, and I continued to feel worse. My abdominal pain did not subside, and my nausea began. Some days, the nausea was so bad that I couldn't eat. I felt like I would vomit at any moment. Thankfully, that was only a day here and there, but it was uncomfortable nonetheless. This led to seeing another specialist and undergoing a lot more testing. It was suspected that I had an abnormal uterus with possible adenomyosis and endometriosis. These discoveries led to a partial hysterectomy in January 2021. Surgery number five. In case you needed a bit of clarity, I had five surgeries in 11 months. That is a lot for the body to endure. I still had a lot of hope for the future and my health issues resolving after that final surgery. I was thankful for that final surgery and believed it was the answer to my health woes.

I wish I could say that resolved my health issues as the doctor and I had hoped, but that simply wasn't the case. I continued to feel worse as my symptoms became more burdensome and widespread. Initially, I wrestled with flu-like symptoms that would come and go unexpectedly. Also, I still dealt with abdominal pain. Prior to this, I truly didn't think I was dealing with anything chronic. Everything I was dealing with seemed to be acute and isolated incidences. However, then I started to have increased nausea, as well as bouts of severe dizziness and general malaise. I have distinct memories of when certain symptoms seemed to be really bad and became a new part of my life because the impact of being unwell is hard to forget. We explored everything—hormonal imbalances, long COVID, GI issues, etc. I spent time in the ER and was admitted to undergo further testing. I had two endoscopies with very minor findings, as well as one colonoscopy.

My symptoms continued to morph, ebb and flow, and grow in number and intensity. I could list at least

40 symptoms I experienced. Sometimes, I only experienced one in a day. Sometimes ten. Other times, I experienced one or two symptoms with great intensity for an entire week. I kept a journal. I wrote down how I felt. I tried a major diet change. I saw a plethora of doctors, every specialty and sub-specialty I could. I went to hematology, hematology-oncology, endocrinology, gastroenterology, integrative medicine, gynecology, and more. I had every test and scan done to rule out anything major. I did X-rays, MRIs, CT scans, PET scans, and blood work, checking every single marker we could think of. I went to Indianapolis to see an amazing IU doctor and Cleveland to see a skilled GI doctor and OBGYN doctor. While every negative test/scan was positive in the eyes of the doctors, it was a punch to the gut for me. I was praying that something, anything, would come back positive so that I could work on a treatment to begin healing. Some tests came back slightly abnormal, but nothing alarming enough to lead to a diagnosis and nothing that explained how horrible my body felt. I tried new

medications, red light therapy, physical therapy, chiropractic care, specialty intensive therapies, and more. All of this was to no avail. My number of symptoms continued to increase, and my hope for healing began to decrease. I went through seasons in which my body was a skeleton. The amount of weight I lost due to being unwell was incredibly unhealthy and seemingly unavoidable. You could see it on my face, and you could see the concern on others' faces as well. I wasn't blind to the reality that I was facing. I was trapped in a body that didn't make a bit of sense to me or any medical professional.

I would love to conclude this chapter by telling you that I have healed physically, but that is not the case. I have slowed down my search for answers. I have accepted that I may be chronically ill forever, but I have NOT given up the fight. While I may not be undergoing extensive testing or seeing a bunch of specialists, I am still trying new protocols and therapies while praying for the Lord to heal my body. As I sit writing this book in the fall of 2024, I am not physically healed. I am learning about what it means to suffer, and I pray that the Lord will make me a redemptive sufferer. Yes, I may suffer, but I want to suffer well in a way that points people to Jesus. I will suffer and fight until I am healed or until I die, but I have hope that one day, I WILL be healed, even if it isn't on this side of heaven. I believe the in restoration of my glorified body. Revelation 21:4 says, "He will wipe away every tear from their eyes, and death shall be no more, neither shall there be mourning, nor crying, nor pain anymore, for the former things have passed away."

This was a part of the journey that those closest to us were aware of. This was also a part of the journey that many people were not aware of. I don't like to say I "hid" it well because that was never my intent. I had babies to raise and a life to live, regardless of how I felt. I wanted to engage in joyful activities and live with joy in all areas of my life. I have always wanted to pour into others and have a heart for serving others without allowing my health to become an excuse. I also knew that stopping the adoption journey because I didn't feel well would likely leave me feeling worse. I would not only terminate the beautiful journey of adoption and the hope of and looking forward to another child, but I would still be sick.

I also wish that this is where I could tell you that we really leaned into God through my illness and that we saw through the devil's scheme to use my health to discourage us. We didn't see this part of the journey as a spiritual attack to deter our adoption, but that is what we believe was happening. Remember me telling you that Satan knows how to attack before he ever does? Well, it is true. He thought that he could attack us via my health and succeed. And through that, our marriage would be negatively impacted as well. I wouldn't go so far as to say that he did succeed, but he got darn close. You see, when we began the adoption process in 2019, I was as healthy as I could be. As you can see, all of that changed in 2020, which could have changed the outcome of our adoption story. As the adoption seemed to be getting nearer and nearer, hope for healing seemed to be getting further and further away from reality.

Challenge/Question for Thought: What kind of opposition do you seem to be facing in your life? How can you see it from a spiritual perspective and respond in a glorifying way?

CHAPTER 4

Surrendering My Will

Hard.

Over the past four years, hard is the word I would use to describe most days of my life. Some are much harder than others. Some are much easier than others. I am not trying, and never was trying, to ignore this reality. Spencer sees it. Some days, the kids really see it. Some days, I am on the verge of tears all day until I finally break down at night. Some days, I have to do as a wise doctor once advised me to do... borrow hope. I know that I have hope in Jesus, but I also have a doctor who believes in my healing, and some days I borrow the hope that he has. This has been true for the past four years due to my health, and it is still true today.

You see, even though I never said it out loud, there were many times throughout the timeline of the adoption I wrestled a lot with questioning if we should adopt. I knew in my heart that it might not be the best idea given the circumstances surrounding my health, but I didn't want to give up on a dream that was so deeply rooted in my heart. Call it stubbornness, if you will, but I know now that it was a God-given tenacity to see the calling through, relying on supernatural strength.

In January 2023, I was at one of the lowest points of my health journey. I had seemingly exhausted all medical resources and dropped a significant amount of weight, all while planning and holding an adoption fundraiser because things seemed to be vamping up on the adoption front. As a result of my condition, I had loving and well-meaning people make comments like, "Are you sure you are healthy enough to go to Africa?" and "I know the adoption seems to be moving, but what about you?" These were genuine concerns from loved ones clouded with fear. I get it. I understand where they were coming from. However, I had come to a place in my faith in which I feared God and God alone. I knew He had brought me to that point in the journey and would see me through it. I had already wrestled with the same questions thrown at me. I wasn't ignoring their concerns, but I had already come to a place of surrender with the Lord, and I wouldn't allow doubt to make me revisit what had already been addressed in my walk with the Lord.

I remember one evening on my living room floor, surrendering the adoption to God. I am sad to say that it took nearly three years for me to come to a place of surrender. It was definitely an issue of my heart not acknowledging the One who gave me the dream in the first place. I questioned what I was doing, and I cried out and said, "God, this adoption story has never been mine. I have made it mine, but it has always been Yours. You placed it on my heart and have used us to pursue it, but I want this to be Your story. If that means we don't adopt, or if we do adopt, make this Your story. I am surrendering this to You, and I will not move forward with this adoption if that is what You desire." That was one of the hardest moments of my life. I wept on my living room floor, crying out to God and releasing my dream (that He gave me) to align with His will.

It made me think back to Abraham in the Bible. He finally had a son, Isaac, who was a miracle from the Lord in Abraham and Sarah's old age. Abraham prayed and waited for his son for so long. And then God told Abraham to sacrifice his only son. So, without hesitation, Abraham goes up a mountain, ties up Isaac, takes out his knife, and prepares to slay his son. "But the angel of the LORD called to him from heaven and said, 'Abraham, Abraham!' And he said, 'Here I am.' He said, '*Do not lay your hand on the boy or do anything to him, for now I know that you fear God, seeing you have not withheld your son, your only son, from me.*'" (Genesis 22:11-12) I believe God wanted to see me release my will to Him. Now, I understand He wasn't asking me to murder my child, but I do think He was doing a heart check to see if I was willing to surrender my child (whom I hadn't met) to Him if that was what He asked me to do. He was saying, "Ashton, are you willing to obey me even when it is hard?" I am so thankful for the gift of that lesson. I am so thankful that He broke me down to surrender to Him completely. It was an eye-opening moment in which I had to confront the sin in my heart— making the adoption less about God's story and more about mine.

The past several years have been refining. God used my health and the adoption to grow me and draw me closer to Himself. In fact, He is still using it to refine my heart. Many evenings, I cry. Many days are hard. Because of my health, I now know God in an experiential way that I did not know Him before. Had I never known what it was like to be truly weak, I would have never known what it meant for Christ to be my strength. I have to rely on Him as my strength daily. Some evenings, sitting in worship to the Lord, I hold joy and thankfulness in one hand while holding pain and anguish in the other. It feels like an irony, but there is something beautifully unexplainable about it.

Many days, I put on a smile and continue because I want to live as normally as possible. But my illness has changed many things. It has changed my ability and desire to commit to plans. It has canceled plans. It has required me to leave locations early because of my physical state. It has led to me asking people to babysit so I can go to yet another appointment that may come up empty. It has looked like forcing myself to eat through the nausea so I don't lose more weight. It has looked like gaining weight when I feel well, so I can afford to lose some weight when I don't. It has looked like standing in the bathroom waiting to vomit and trash cans at my bedside when I don't have the flu. It has often left me in a state of "when will this flare end?" knowing it may never end at all.

Suffering is interesting. When I was healthy, I could say that I relied on Jesus everyday, but did I really? I ran around, worked out, stayed busy, and went about life without thinking twice about it. It made me feel like I had everything under control and relied on myself to function. When physical suffering enters, things change. I realize that I CAN'T do it on my own. I realize I never did it on my own at all. I had good health, and the Lord sustained me daily before. Now, my health has been stripped from me, and the Lord still sustains me daily. Now, I pray for Him to sustain me and thank Him for the good days. Now, I am fully aware of my need for Him. For that, I am thankful. That is a gift.

You know what else is a gift? Napping with my son, Liam. When I was healthy, I didn't necessarily NEED to nap. I would lay Liam down to rest while I went about managing the household. Now, when Liam needs a nap, I often lie down with him. I cherish these moments. Liam will intertwine his little fingers with mine, throw his legs on top of mine, and wrap his arms around me. Sometimes, when I catch him still with his eyes open, he flashes me the sweetest and orneriest grin. These moments in time are forever engrained in my mind. I have these moments because I am sick. Because I feel like I have to nap. For that, I am also thankful.

It has often been easy to let my mind say, "This isn't the mom my children should have. They were never meant to have a mom who struggles daily to give her best, but it just doesn't feel like enough. They deserve who I used to be, full of energy and involvement." But I know that is the devil talking. God KNEW this was the mother my children would have long before I did. I was never promised an easy life free from suffering. I am exactly who God knew I would be since the beginning. The reality in raising my children is that now I sometimes snap at them in the store because my symptoms hit me so hard that I struggle to control my reactions, and then I apologize to them at bedtime for the sin exposed in my adversity. My health does not give me an excuse to sin, and I am thankful that my children forgive me over and over again. Now, I struggle to get up and dance with them in the living room some evenings because my symptoms are overwhelming. I feel like I am robbing them of a "normal" mom. But this is the normal mom they know and the one God prepared for them since the beginning. Instead of allowing my health to define me as a good or bad mom, I have to let the Bible define what that looks like. Dancing with vigor in the living room or chasing my kids around the park aren't requirements for being a good mom. Learning how to become more like Jesus through God's Word is the measuring stick to being a good mom. Allowing God to show me my sin in response to my struggles and asking for forgiveness is humbling for me, and it allows my children to see that I am still in the process of sanctification. I can acknowledge that my suffering has become that of my husband and children as well. If I don't suffer gracefully, how will they?

Can I be really vulnerable for a moment? I have had thoughts such as, "I know God wants me to be a good mom, but that is hard to do when I struggle with health so intensely. Why doesn't He heal me so I can be a good mom to my children?" There was

43

a truth within that thought. Being a good mom has been so hard when my health has bogged me down. However, instead of acknowledging that truth and running to scripture, I questioned God instead of examining my heart. I was the issue, not God. I have wrestled with patience and self-control when I feel poor. Is my health at fault? No! My health has exposed my heart and areas in which I need to repent and grow. Maybe God hasn't healed me because He still wants to refine me. Of course, that may not be the reason, but I am choosing to allow my health to expose my heart to sanctify my life. The Lord has taught me that I don't have to be healed physically in order to be a good mom.

I have laid in bed many nights after a long, hard day and prayed, "Lord, if this is the rest of my life, I'm okay if you take me today. I'm fine if I don't wake up in the morning because I am weary and don't feel like I can fight anymore." I share this out of vulnerability that maybe my situation and desperation resonate with one of you. I want you to know that you are not alone. I also want you to know

44

that God sees you. Trust that there is a reason you aren't healed (physically, relationally, mentally, or likewise). More importantly, trust that God has a daily purpose for your life. He places the breath in your lungs each moment you breathe, so He wakes you up with great purpose.

I had a wise counselor tell me it was time to say goodbye to who I once was. This felt like an impossibly hard task at the time. But he was right. There have been many times throughout the last several years in which I have mourned the person I used to be. I grieved the life I used to live. However, I grieved while also wishing I was still that person. Saying goodbye is different, though; it is laying down the old me and not wishing for that girl back. It is accepting and embracing the person the Lord has made me to be due to the hard things I have experienced. Sure, I can't work out like I once did— daily and with vigor. I don't dance in the living room with my kids—full of the energy I once had. I may wrestle through simple, everyday tasks sometimes. I may not clean the house as often as I like or as thoroughly as I used to. However, who I now am at heart is full of more depth, full of more compassion for others, and desires to know Jesus more. I can say goodbye to who I was and be thankful for who I am. I can now trust that the Lord will use everything for my growth and His glory.

I grew up with a great life. And I still have a great life. Growing up, though, I never experienced HARD. Of course, I had woes, trials, and disappointments. I experienced letdowns, tears, and pain. And if I am honest, many of my struggles were a result of my own bad choices and immaturity. But, I never experienced life-changing, heart-crushing HARD. I am thankful I grew up with the life I had free from significant hardship, but I am also thankful for this season of growth. I wouldn't be who I am or know Jesus like I do if it weren't for this season. I find myself fighting my flesh when I may want to fall back on feeling sorry for myself or complaining about my situation. I fight because my heart knows the truth of who God is and how good He is. I have to remind myself that He is truly in control. He wouldn't be allowing me to go through what I am experiencing if He didn't have a purpose for it.

John 16:33 says, "I have said these things to you, that in me you may have peace. *In the world you will have tribulation. But take heart; I have overcome the world.*" I don't know how this verse resonates with you, but initially, it provokes fear in my heart. We are told that we will have struggles in this life. However, we are also given the promise of Jesus in this world. He is our Comforter through the tribulation. The last part of that verse simply can't be ignored. Nobody wants to experience challenges that may rock their world, and I am no exception. However, this verse doesn't say "if" you have tribulation. Hard times are unavoidable. And quite frankly, I believe that God allowed me to be inflicted in this way for a reason. I won't claim to know God's full intentions because we serve a mysterious God, but we can be sure He knows what He is doing, even when we can't see it.

James 1:2-4 says, "Count it all joy, my brothers when you meet trials of various kinds, for you know that the testing of your faith produces steadfastness. And let steadfastness have its full effect, that you may be perfect and complete, lacking in nothing." I did a Bible study on the book of James, which shed great light on this passage. The author of the study talks about how the work of God through the trials we face is much like the work of a silversmith. A silversmith heats silver until the impurities rise to the top so that they can remove the imperfections. They continue removing the imperfections until they are gone, and the silversmith can see their own reflection in the silver. In the same way, I pray and believe God is using my health trials to show me my own sins and impurities so He can remove them and see Himself in me. I pray that I can receive his purification work humbly and gracefully.

Challenge/Question for Thought: Are you holding onto something with tight fists that you need to surrender to God? How can you allow your trials to purify your heart and become closer to Jesus?

CHAPTER 5

For Better or For Worse

"I…take thee… to be my wedded wife/husband. To have and to hold from this day forward. For better, for worse, for richer, for poorer. In sickness and in health. To love and to cherish. Till death do us part." All who are married have said these vows or some variation of them. They are traditional vows, and they are intentionally-worded vows. Of course, we would never leave our spouse because they get sick. Of course, we would never leave them because we aren't making enough money. We would never dare leave them when life becomes "worse." But the reality is that when we want to leave our spouse, the issue runs much deeper than sickness, money, or hardship. The issue always goes back to the heart. The issue can expose itself as stress around finances, one person feeling stressed about picking up the sick partner's workload, etc. Nevertheless, if we actually analyze the situation, it runs much deeper than circumstantial stress or happiness. It is pretty easy to make these vows when staring into the eyes of the one you love deeply on your wedding day. It is much harder to live them out day-to-day when the rubber meets the road, and life gets hard. In fact, I think it is easy to forget we said these things in the first place. If we truly remembered the vow and commitment we made, we wouldn't be so quick to abandon our words when life gets tough. I'll be the first to raise my hand when they say guilty as charged.

As my health took a drastic turn for the worse, my marriage with Spencer was also on the rocks. The reality is that it had been declining as quickly as the rate of my health; we just didn't realize it. We lived life in a state of day-in, day-out, survival mode. We lived life going through the motions. We took care of the kids, worked, got involved with social commitments, and made time to even go on dates occasionally. Those things are part of life for everyone. However, we don't realize the danger in what we are doing until it becomes seemingly too late, and we have drifted so far apart that we can't seem to find a way forward together anymore. None of the things we were doing were bad. However, as we did the day-in and day-out, we stopped focusing on our marriage, starving it of the attention it deserved. We were active members in our church, involved in a Bible study, and yet, not one person knew the state or struggles of our marriage. The one place we should have felt most able to confess, share, and rely on others is one of the places we chose not to open up.

As we did daily life, I was also seeing doctors, changing diets, trying new therapies, and stressed about the state of my body. Spencer was working hard to provide for our needs and pay medical bills, which added up quickly. Our communication about the circumstances surrounding our lives was surface-level as I explored ways to improve my health, and he let me do that. Exploring my health and him allowing me to do that was not wrong, but not keeping the channels of communication open and honest along the way led to years of anger, resentment, doubt, and pride.

You see, Spencer and I were both wrestling with some really hard feelings. We had many thoughts swirling around in our hearts and heads, and there was seemingly no way to express them. Wrestling with them wasn't the issue, but we wrestled alone, allowing Satan to twist the thoughts in our minds and pit us against each other. Satan is really good at taking truths and twisting them enough to become untruths. If we aren't guarding our minds, the untruths can take hold in our hearts. I will be the first to admit that I was not actively seeking out the Lord in this area of life as my source of comfort and truth.

Among other things, we specifically had doubts and fears about my health and moving forward with the adoption. I didn't want to express my doubt and fear to him because I could tell he was already apprehensive before he ever expressed it. The body language and side comments were enough indication. I thought, "If I tell him how I feel, it will confirm how he feels, and then he will no longer want to continue the adoption process." Spencer didn't want to express his fear because he didn't want to crush my dream, make me feel worse on top of my health issues, and was apprehensive of my reaction. Isn't that scenario so sad? We had such similar thoughts that could have brought us closer together if we had approached the situation in a healthy manner. Instead, we wrestled alone, allowing Satan to work hard tearing our marriage apart. Realistically, if we had both been open and honest about our feelings, we could have wrestled with the doubt together and come to a place of connection instead of drifting further apart.

Let me break it down really simply. My pride said, "If I tell Spencer, I won't get my way." Isn't it so like Satan to plant thoughts in our heads that fester and grow into something bigger? I allowed Satan to win that battle in my mind. If I listened to the truth of God's word and trusted my husband's heart, I would have been able to lovingly approach him with my fear and doubt and allow him to handle it delicately as we made decisions going forward. Now, there are reasons why I felt like I couldn't do that, but that isn't the point. There were reasons why Spencer felt like he couldn't approach me, either. We all know it takes two to tango, but I can only speak for myself, share the sin in my heart, repent, and rely on the Spirit to become more like Jesus.

As my health was at its lowest in January 2023, that is also when everything mentioned so far came to a head in our marriage. In fact, the tension was so palpable that being in our house was uncomfortable. That was nearly four years into the journey of adoption and nearly three years into my health journey, so a lot had built up over time. I had started planning another adoption fundraiser in the fall of 2022 to take place in January 2023. I did every bit of the work to make it happen, with the help of family and friends and local businesses, but

I can tell you Spencer did not participate. Please hear me. I am not bashing him or blaming him. I don't say that to make him look bad, or me look good. It goes to show you where his mind and my heart were. He was wrestling so badly, without ever expressing it, that maybe the adoption shouldn't happen because of my health. He didn't want to jump all-in on yet another fundraiser if stopping the adoption process was the next inevitable thing to happen. And honestly, my heart knew that and struggled with that same thought, but I ignored it, unwilling to open up that conversation with my husband. I had hoped that the answer to my health would still come, and I had a trip planned to Cleveland Clinic to explore more possibilities. Even if the answer didn't come, I still didn't feel like God was closing the door on the adoption.

All of the ill feelings and lack of hard conversations were taking a toll on our marriage without us ever acknowledging it. Everything came to a head one evening when divorce felt like the only option we had, and we discussed it mutually as a very real possibility. To show you how Satan works, the fight that "did it" for me was the result of dinner being poorly received. Obviously, the issue was MUCH deeper than that, but we didn't know how to flesh it out. We had even talked about how divorce could be a civil thing that we both agreed to. We felt like life was taking us in different directions, and we didn't know how to remedy that and move forward together. It was as if we disagreed on everything. And realistically, we kind of did disagree on everything, from how my health was playing out, how we should raise the kids, how we tithe, to which church to attend after leaving a situation that hurt us, etc. We both felt like we were restricting each other from pursuing areas God was calling us to. But you know what God was ultimately calling us to? Himself and each other.

If there is one thing I am sure of, it is that God was not calling us to a life of divorce and a family ripped apart. That is not His design and intention for marriage. Two people rooted in Christ and working together as a team CAN disagree on things but still compromise, love each other deeply, and continue in a positive direction. Disagreement does not mean that the marriage must end so we can pursue our selfish desires. That sounds like an obvious statement as I put my pen to paper, but that was really what we were considering in the near future. Leave each other to pursue what each of us wanted individually. I can promise you that is not the vow we gave on our wedding day.

I sometimes wonder what healing may have looked like had we kept open and honest communication throughout the past several years instead of bottling everything up all that time. However, I am not living in the "what if?" I am choosing to use the situation to allow God to change my heart and help me grow and learn as a Christian, wife, and mother. Looking back, the narrative is much clearer than when going through the thick of our issues. Do you see it? Satan pitted Spencer and me against each other, convincing us to view each other as the enemy when the real enemy was Satan all along. We did not see it at the time, but thankfully, we could lean into trained counselors who brought a fresh perspective on the foundation of what was happening in our marriage.

Challenge/Question for Thought: If you are married, are you struggling to remember and keep your vows? How can you stop to consider what role you play or what action you can take to improve the current situation by addressing the root issue? If you are single, what ideas of marriage do you hold that may be untrue in regard to a spouse making you happy, filling a need in your life, etc.? Or, how can you prepare yourself for marriage by leaning into being a better Christian first?

CHAPTER 6

A Lesson in Counseling

Enter counseling. It was a last-ditch effort, but an effort nonetheless. Spencer and I knew that jumping into counseling was necessary if there was any hope for healing in our marriage. We had tried counseling a year or so into our journey, knowing that we needed something, but the counseling we received at the time was poor and shallow, which Spencer and I both agreed was not in line with what we needed. We still wanted to explore options but came up empty on good counseling that we could afford, so we halted seeking help. Unlike us, I would recommend that you don't wait. Don't wait until things get to the point of needing emergency counselors like we did. Find something for the in-between moments. I believe that seeking counsel, individually or as a couple, is beneficial in any stage of life. Many verses talk about the counsel we have in Jesus. Psalm 73:24 says, "You guide me with your counsel, and afterward you will receive me to glory." We serve a wonderful Counselor, and He has gifted others with a similar skillset.

In January 2023, we found a Christian organization that offered counseling for any area of life that was more affordable than others we had come across. We were able to share our concerns and issues so they could match us with counselors who would be the best fit given our circumstances. Soon after, we began seeing a couple who seemed the perfect fit for us. The couple dealt with a chronically ill wife, church hurt, and many other areas with which we struggled.

The path of counseling through this specific organization was focused on emotions. We worked with the couple on discussing our experiences through the lens of how each situation made us feel. This gave Spencer and I both an avenue that allowed us to express all of the built-up hurt in our hearts. While this taught us a lot about emotions and helped us communicate what we were feeling and had been struggling with, I knew in my heart it wasn't the right fit for us. This was a Christian organization, but the counseling was not inherently biblical. My heart yearned for something much better and deeper than what we were experiencing. Throughout the few months of counseling, I consistently expressed my concerns surrounding unbiblical teachings but continued anyway, hoping things would improve. After a few months, I expressed my desire to end counseling (with this particular couple), and even that brought about issues in our marriage. We were not in agreement on the need to end the sessions. My heart longed for deep, biblical truth as the basis for our counseling. Ending this particular counseling was not exposing a heart unwilling to change or unwilling to work on our marriage. Sadly, I felt so much shame choosing to step away from the counseling because it was not a joint decision or one the counselors agreed with. I had expressed my concerns and made the decision to end the sessions, knowing the spiritual growth that we needed was not happening. Not only were we stagnant in our spiritual growth, but we weren't healing maritally because the root of our issues wasn't being addressed. The conviction in my heart to end counseling drove me and Spencer further apart.

In the fall of 2023, we began seeing a new counselor to continue to work on our marriage. The counselor had great intentions to help and see us heal. This particular counselor was also a Christian, but again, his counseling was anything but biblical. His focus was on our past. He spent a lot of time talking about our parents, our upbringing, and our experiences. Every week, we spent time talking about the emotions we felt surrounding our lived experiences. This form of counseling has benefits. I think that we need to figure out some of our tendencies based on how we were raised and the things we experienced. This can be helpful in explaining why we do certain things. However, our past does not define us. And, if we claim to be Christians, we are NEW creations with the power of the spirit in us to create change. 2 Corinthians 5:17 says, "Therefore, if anyone is in Christ, he is a new creation. The old has passed away; behold the new has come."

Session after session, we continued with the same narrative. We shared our concerns for our marriage and spent time discussing my health. After just a few meetings together, the counselor advised us to put a hold on our adoption for the time being. Mind you, we had already accepted a match for our son and planned to leave for Ghana as soon as we received the Article 5, which was imminent. We didn't know it that particular day he made the recommendation, but he advised us to put the adoption on hold one month before we actually took flight to Ghana. Upon hearing those words of advice, Spencer felt a sense of being seen but felt it was an awkward recommendation given the timing of the adoption. He had felt similar at an earlier point in the adoption process. In fact, if this recommendation had come about nine months earlier, we may have given more thought to the idea, even though I still am not sure how well received those words would have been. Because the adoption was taking so long, Spencer had previously felt that maybe that was a way of the Lord closing the door on the adoption since my health still wasn't resolved.

What really got me was the reason for the advice. It came from a place of telling me I had too much anxiety. The counselor was looking at my past and prescribing anxiety to be the reason we should close the door on the adoption. He mentioned that my anxiety would only get worse by adding another child to the mix. Don't get me wrong, I think that can happen. But Satan used that situation to speak anxiety into my life that didn't exist prior. I allowed the counselor's well-meaning advice to have more merit in my heart than God's word.

The day after that conversation, I nearly had a mental breakdown. I sobbed and sobbed while my body shook with fear and panic. I had already released the adoption to the Lord and my willing surrender if that was what the Lord desired...and now this. I had no idea what to do with this new information. I spent a lot of time in prayer, sought counsel, and leaned into God's Word and other biblical resources on anxiety. I also had some really great friends speak truth into my life. I came out on the other side of the situation, realizing I allowed someone to speak something into my life that wasn't true. Satan used my health to impact our marriage, which brought us to counseling, which nearly halted the meeting of our son.

Initially, I was angry with this counselor. I could sit and mull over what happened, but I chose to use this as an opportunity for growth. This was a great learning experience in which the spiritual warfare became increasingly obvious as we approached the adoption. It took the previous four years of opposition to bring us to this. I do remember hanging up from that video session and instantly saying, "I think we are experiencing spiritual warfare." It is crazy to look back and realize it took me up to this moment to truly see the battle we were facing. I guess you could say this was the final straw that prompted me to question our experiences. This is also why it is important to take every thought captive and make our thoughts obedient to Christ. 2 Corinthians 10:5 says, "We destroy arguments and every lofty opinion raised against the knowledge of God, and *take every thought captive to obey Christ.*" I messed this one up big time. We were following through with the adoption in obedience to what Christ called us to. I should have taken my thoughts captive instead of ruminating on the lies spoken to me.

Because the adoption took off soon after this session, we only had one or two more sessions before heading to Ghana and ending counseling yet again. We knew and agreed that seeing this counselor was no longer beneficial either. He kept us talking in circles about our past and how we felt.

We don't believe his goal was ever to get us OUT of our need for counseling. We were paying him to feel validated in our experiences but never to find healing or see marital issues resolved. Thankfully, we weren't giving up hope on our marriage at this point, but we did had to put a pause on counseling due to the arrangements of our journey to Ghana. We did not know what was in store for our marriage, the healing still needing to take place, or how that would happen going forward. We had our sights set on Africa and all the required details for that endeavor. Thankfully, the Lord had set better plans in motion for us that revealed themselves while in Ghana for the adoption.

Challenge/Question for Thought: What do you need help with that counseling may be able to assist in? What is holding you back from seeking help? Are you allowing Satan to use people to speak mistruths in your life?

CHAPTER 7

A Match at Last

People often don't understand why international adoption takes so long, especially in African countries. During my time in Ghana, I learned a lot about this, and some of the information is truly heartbreaking. While there are so many orphaned children in Ghana, only a certain number are actually adoptable. Social workers have to go to great lengths to ensure that the children being orphaned no longer have any living relatives who want to care for them. This seems like it would be fairly straightforward, but Ghana is considered a developing nation. They don't often have things documented nicely in organized systems. They don't have a good record to keep track of where people live or if they move. Addresses aren't commonly used in Ghana, as people rely on landmarks to give them an idea of where someone is located. The other major contributing factor in determining a child's adoptability is poverty. We were told a story of a kid who was at an orphanage with no family to claim him. He had been there many years. They went to search for his mom but were informed she died. They had a death certificate, a record of a funeral taking place, and seemingly legitimate evidence she died. They went to her village, and friends and family confirmed her death. Ready for the kicker? The mother wasn't dead at all. She went to such lengths as faking her death because she was too poor to raise her child. She took him to an orphanage where he would be taken care of and fed daily. Ultimately, that child wasn't adoptable. Can you imagine feeling so desperate for your child to have a shot at life that you fake your own death?

As white people coming to Ghana to adopt, we stood out in public, and we quickly understood how taboo it was to be doing what we were. If we were out and about with our son, we would get a lot of odd looks. Some seemed angry, while others seemed confused. When talking to our friends, who were locals, we learned that adoption is hardly a thought in the mind of most Ghanaians. Many people in Ghana are struggling to make ends meet daily, with enough children of their own. They were not in a place to even consider adoption a thing, even if it was their own kin. So, the odd looks we received typically came from a place of curiosity. Funny enough, we also got many questions from ex-pats from different nations. People have a hard time understanding why a family with three children already would want to adopt more children, especially considering the cost and sacrifice required. This lack of understanding opened many doors for us to share the gospel and our hearts for our children. It also opened our eyes to the reality that many locals face when presented the opportunity to possibly adopt their own kin and then the time it takes to determine a child's adoptability.

It seems evident that Satan was really trying to put an end to our adoption through the timing of everything. Again, he is always prowling, waiting to devour whatever he can. Even more specifically, Satan wants to destroy the family. Satan was working hard while we waited to be matched with a child, aiming to end our marriage and plant seeds of doubt surrounding the timing of my health. A family being fruitful for the Kingdom of God is contrary to Satan's goals in this world. However, we serve a God who came so that we "may have life and have it abundantly," according to John 10:10. By keeping our sights on the God we serve, we prevent Satan from claiming any sort of victory in our lives. Years went by, and we were not being placed with a child to call our own. The conversation had come up briefly to possibly only give the process a little bit more time before we decided to end that chapter in our lives. We almost put an end date to the time we were willing to wait to receive a match as Spencer thought maybe this was God's way of closing the door on adoption, as previously mentioned.

From the beginning of the adoption process, we had an approved home study to adopt a boy or girl (or two if available), ages 0-3 years. I never cared about the gender of the child. I always thought I wanted a younger kid because that meant it would be easier. It would mean less time for trauma to happen in a child's life and less time for them to grow up without a family. I have since learned that that thought process is extremely flawed. Some younger children are much more difficult but certainly not always. The reason can't be known exactly, but each child responds to trauma and attachment issues differently. I also had high hopes of adopting two kids at once. When we mentioned the idea to our adoption agency, they said that most people who want to adopt two kids at the same time can do that. I was fully anticipating that based on the agency's comment. It is also much more affordable to adopt two kids simultaneously than to go through the adoption process twice, which had been a consideration. However, we were struggling to get a match at all and started feeling discouraged in our journey.

In late 2022, we received a copy of a waiting child list. This was a document compiled of kids who were immediately available for adoption that the agency in Ghana was advocating to find homes for. 2022 was the first time we knew of a list like this, and I am so thankful it was sent our way. On that list was a three-year-old boy waiting for a family. He was almost four, so we had to consider if we wanted to adjust our parameters to the child we would adopt. After some prayer and conversation, we decided to update our home study to reflect an age range of 0-5 so we could begin to pursue this child. After the new approval and us expressing our interest, the agency sent us all the details they could on a little four-year-old boy named Kwadwo Bismark in April of 2023. Without seeing his face or hearing his voice, we were able to review his file, compiled with his medical information and what little of his background was known, take it to medical professionals, and pray over the decision to accept or deny the matching of this little boy to our family.

In May of 2023, we officially accepted the match of our little boy. At that time, we received pictures of him and a short video of him at school. To say that I was swooning would be an understatement. We finally had the name and face of the child we had prayed for so long. Unbeknownst to Kwadwo Bismark, he was born about one month before a couple from a small town in Indiana filled out an application to begin the adoption process. Not only that, but as the waiting grew harder and closing the door seemed nearer, his profile appeared on a piece of paper to be considered. When I think about a little boy born in Kumasi, Ghana, and a simple family living in Northeast Indiana, I am awestruck at the miracle of the joining together of these lives. Just like we pursued Kwadwo Bismark years before he (or we) even realized it, God pursued our hearts long before we ever were aware.

The Bible offers a lot of words on Jesus' pursuit of us. Ezekiel 34:11 says, "For thus says the Lord God: Behold, I, I myself will search for my sheep and will seek them out." Then, in Luke 19:10, Jesus says, "For the Son of Man came to seek and to save the lost." I don't know about you, but I am so thankful for this reality. Even when I am running from Jesus, He continues to pursue me. Our pursuit of our son is only a glimpse into what that looks like. Kwadwo Bismark had no idea that we were pursuing him for years until the Lord aligned our paths. Likewise, we don't see the lengths that Jesus goes to pursue our hearts, but we can be confident He does.

The huge step in the journey to be matched with a child took place a little over four years after beginning the adoption process. Over time, changes happen within adoption programs that have major life implications, and Ghana was no exception. As the time waiting went on, the requirements for time in the country changed. When we first agreed to join the Ghana program, it was required that we stay in the country for one month to bond, come home while waiting for paperwork to process for several months, and then go back for a second trip for approximately two weeks to go to court and then bring our adopted child home. At the time, we were hoping that only one of us would have to leave Ghana between the two required trips, as leaving the child we had bonded with would be emotionally challenging for both us as the parents and the child. We also thought about the flights and the added expense of going back and forth. It made the most sense to stay if one of us could. However, these were all hypothetical scenarios because we had no idea how we would make that work with our schedules and biological children. The longer time went on and we waited to be matched with a child, the requirements changed to a four-month stay in the country to do everything necessary and then bring the child home. So, we were left with no other option.

For us, staying in Ghana for four months did not make sense logistically or financially. It certainly was never part of our plan. However, we didn't question IF we would do that. We knew it was what had to be done for our child. Think of your children. Is there anything you wouldn't do to reach them and bring them home if separated from you? Of course not! We felt the same way about our Kwadwo Bismark. This was one of the details in our story in which I had to go back to Proverbs 3:5. "Trust in the Lord with all your heart, and do not lean on your own understanding." This verse is important because our hearts are fickle, and our emotions will lead us astray. I certainly did not understand the new plan set before us, which is why we had to lean on the One who cares so deeply for us—the One we can trust.

Maybe there is something in your life that you can't see how things could play out in the future. Nevertheless, trust in the Lord. Maybe you said "yes" to something that the Lord wants you to pursue, but now you are waiting for further confirmation from Him to begin the pursuit. I encourage you not to wait. Rather, boldly step into what God has for you. Our humanness thrives in knowing what will happen and when—it gives us a sense of control. We want to be able to predict the next steps so we can be comfortable and prepare accordingly. However, I encourage you to trust that God will make a way for you regardless of your circumstances. Proverbs 16:9 says, "The heart of man plans his way, but the Lord establishes his steps." Be obedient to God without knowing the details because the Bible tells us that the Lord establishes our steps anyway. We did not have the option to wait for confirmation to continue pursuing the adoption. For better or for worse, we were all in and had to trust God to bring us through the four-month journey we never planned ourselves.

Challenge/Question for Thought: Is there an area in your life where you said "yes" to the Lord but are waiting for further confirmation? If so, what is holding you back from trusting the Lord to prepare your path? In what area of your life do you need to surrender and fully put your trust in Jesus?

CHAPTER 8

An African Adventure Begins

The time had finally come. After spending hours upon hours packing and prepping to move overseas for four months, it was time to head to Africa. I was equally excited as I was nervous. I knew in the grand scheme of life that four months is hardly any time at all. I also knew that being out of our comfort zone, adding a member to the family, staying healthy in a developing country, protecting our family, and navigating a new way of life in a new environment would be nothing to scoff at. But, on Thanksgiving Day 2023, Spencer and I started on the trek of a lifetime with lessons and memories awaiting our future. It was surreal that the call to Africa was finally coming to fruition after all the time that had passed since beginning the adoption journey.

The travel days to and from Ghana were long. We drove to Chicago, flew to New York, had a layover, and then flew to Accra, Ghana's capital city. The flight time was a little over ten hours, but the total travel time was closer to 24 hours when you add in drive time, arriving early, the layover, etc. Upon arriving in Ghana, the country was five hours ahead of America. It is safe to say that we were exhausted and hungry upon landing (we all know how airplane food tastes). Not only that, but I was overcome with emotion. Something hit me. As soon as Spencer and I landed and had a driver take us to our apartment, a well of emotions poured out of me and onto Spencer's sleeve. Panic and doubt took over as we were thousands of miles from home without our children or any other family or friends that we loved. There was so much unknown waiting ahead of us. I was also having fear about my health. If something went wrong, I was outside the comfort of American healthcare systems.

We didn't know it at the time (thankfully), but even the emergency services in Ghana were unreliable. Some friends we met there later told us the story of an ambulance arriving at the scene of an emergency to transport someone to the hospital. The ambulance driver then informed the patient that he would need to pay for gas to get to the hospital. I was mind-blown when we heard about this. Both corruption and poverty at multiple levels deprived some people of life-saving care like we have access to in America. It would sometimes happen that people died needlessly as a result of systems such as that one.

We had tried to prepare for our first evening in Ghana as well as possible before arriving. A few other adoptive families were in Ghana already (and had been for a long time), so we took any tips we could get from them. Bottled water was waiting for us, thanks to our apartment complex, and a friend told us about an app we could use to have food delivered right to our door. Our first Ghanaian meal? Kentucky Fried Chicken....minus the mashed potatoes. They serve fries over there as the side, which was a major disappointment to me.

As a result of the anxiety that I was feeling, I couldn't eat much of the food once it arrived anyway.

The emotion I experienced was my first dose of the reality of how helpless I truly am outside of Christ. I had no control, which is a hard place to be. Control really is a false perception that we carry. We think we have so much control over our daily lives, but we have a God who holds everything in His hands. That particular evening was an eye-opener as to how little control I actually have in any area of my life. Honestly, I am so thankful that God, who created me, has the final say in my life. Because of our vulnerability in that moment, I felt a sense of the ability (albeit forced) to surrender my perceived control and allow myself to trust in God fully. Had I never truly lost all control, I would never have known and experienced God as the sovereign Ruler of my life.

The Lord also placed some amazing people in our lives during that season. The day after landing in Ghana, we linked up with another adoptive family to show us around and help us feel welcomed and more comfortable. I will never forget the gratitude I felt toward that adoptive mom for showing up with her son to ease our concerns and help us acclimate. We serve a God who cares about the simple things, such as where to grocery shop in a foreign country, and provides people in our path to meet those needs.

As you may have noticed, Spencer and I embarked on the journey without our children, which we felt best considering the plan we had in place. We planned to acclimate ourselves in the area of Accra where we were staying, get groceries, find the local places to shop, etc., and then travel to meet our son. About a week later, my parents would land in Accra with our children to spend time bonding. We had great intentions of meeting our son and bringing him back to the apartment without the overwhelming feeling of meeting all his siblings and having multiple people speaking to him in a foreign language in a completely unfamiliar home.

Prior to traveling, we were told to plan on flying out as soon as we received a document called the Article 5. Once we had that, we would be good to go. So that was what we did. We booked travel within three weeks of receiving that document. When we left for Ghana, we were under the impression that we would get to travel to Kumasi within a week or less of landing in the country. Kumasi was the orphanage's location where we would meet our son and pick him up to bring him back to our apartment in Accra. Little did we know, God had a different plan for us.

After settling into our apartment, walking around the area, and getting some basic supplies to stock our living area, we awaited the go-ahead to travel to Kumasi. Much to our surprise, we did not have all the necessary documentation to make the trek to the orphanage the following Monday. We needed two letters: a letter from the Central Adoption Authority (CAA), the head of all adoptions in Ghana, and a letter from the head of the Department of Social Welfare in Kumasi. This sounded like a fairly straightforward task to complete, but it was anything but simple. From our experience in Ghana, some people would decide when they would show up to work and how much work they would do once there. We experienced some locals not going to work because it was Friday, because it was raining, or for other reasons in between. We also quickly realized how many holidays in Ghana were observed and how much time people would take off accordingly. I am sharing this to give context to our situation and how truly difficult it was for us to conduct business in Ghana. Spencer and I waited and waited and waited for the letters. We waited for days upon end. We were given updates on when we may be able to expect the letters, only to be let down.

I will be honest when I say that our time felt like a waste in one sense. We were eating into Spencer's limited FMLA. We had no money coming in and were spending money to live in Ghana while paying bills back home. The cost of living in our area was incredibly high as we were very close to the US Embassy. The rent price was astronomical, as it was nearly three times more than our mortgage back home. The groceries we were used to back home far exceeded their prices due to them being imported. We missed our children dearly and had moved no further in the adoption process than when we had left for Accra. Not only that, but we also did not know WHEN we could travel to Kumasi. Spencer and I were angry and helpless. What happened to us could have been avoided entirely. In fact, we later learned that those letters we needed could have been obtained months earlier before we traveled while we were waiting for the Article 5.

While it was easy to feel like that time waiting may have been a waste, I absolutely do not view those days like that as I reflect on them. It was just more challenging to keep that perspective in the moment. We met some amazing people (specifically other adoptive families) with whom we got to spend precious time. We slept off the severe jet lag that seemed to take a while to adjust to. We played games, watched shows, and enjoyed each other's company. I also felt a sense of peace in the Lord like never before. While our family was despairing on our behalf thousands of miles away, I felt a sense of calm and trust. Yes, we were angry, but it didn't lead us to despair, although it could have. The calm that I felt is something that truly could only come from the Lord. Because of the chaos of the situation, I was able to get to know God as the Prince of Peace.

Psalm 23 is one of the most well-known passages in the Bible. It is easy to recite without reflection, but I believe it carries great significance and teaching when we truly meditate on the meaning. "The Lord is my shepherd; I shall not want. He makes me lie down in green pastures. He leads me beside still waters. He restores my soul. He leads me in paths of righteousness for his name's sake. Even though I walk through the valley of the shadow of death, I will fear no evil, for you are with me; your rod and your staff, they comfort me. You prepare a table for me in the presence of my enemies; you anoint my head with oil; my cup overflows. Surely goodness and mercy shall follow me all the days of my life, and I shall dwell in the house of the Lord forever."

David was experiencing a tough time in his life as he says, "I walk through the valley of the shadow of death," but his heart remained steadfast, and his hope was in the Lord. He did not allow his circumstances to bring him to despair. The Lord provided for him *in the presence* of his enemies. The Lord did not remove David from his enemies, and therefore, David felt comfort in a place of safety. No! He found comfort in the One who guided him in the midst of darkness. I pray that this can be my heart posture in every situation I face and not just this one instance from our adoption story. To be honest, I have failed at this heart posture many times over the past several years. I have lost sight of the Shepherd, allowing the Enemy to have a say over my heart and mind. I have had many moments of questioning God, not acknowledging His presence, and not giving Him glory through my challenging circumstances.

After 15 long days, the same day my parents and the kids were hopping on a plane to join us, we received word that our contacts on the ground in Ghana had received the long-awaited letter from the CAA on December 8, 2023. Also, the director in Kumasi permitted us to go to the orphanage. That landed on a Friday, so we knew we would have to wait until at least Monday to travel to the orphanage. We had some travel logistics to work out at that point in time, but ready or not, we would soon be joined by five more family members, ready to embark on the journey to Kumasi to meet a boy who would change our world. We were blessed by how things transpired because the Lord had the perfect timing in His control.

Challenge/Question for Thought: In what area of your life do you have a hard time letting go of control? What makes your heart desire that control, and how can you surrender that to the Lord?

CHAPTER 9

Meeting Our Son

Meeting our sweet boy, who was called "Bismark" by those who knew him, was a beautifully special experience that feels most appropriate to share with everyone. There is some mystery and probably a lot of misconceptions about how that meeting happens. In fact, the meeting of a child with their adoptive parents for the first time looks different for everyone due to many variables. I know so many people would love insight, so I will share our experience as an example. In doing so, I will share my journal entries on the particular day we met Bismark and then the day we took him to live with us. Three days after landing in Accra, my parents and kids (surely exhausted as could be) joined Spencer and me on the eventful and whirlwind journey to Bismark's orphanage in Kumasi, Ghana.

The following are the journal entries from the days of meeting and bringing Bismark "home" after twenty days in Ghana. The journals have been tweaked and revised to include more details about our experience.

December 12, 2023

"Our day started bright and early. We woke at 4:30 am for a driver to pick us up at 5:00 am to begin our day. We packed some bags in the 15-passenger van (with much-needed AC), headed to pick up our social worker, and began our journey to Kumasi. We were headed out on the adventure of a lifetime. We were told the drive was four to five hours, depending on the driver. That same drive in America would probably only take two hours. However, the roads in Ghana are no joke. I have never felt bumps like what I felt on that trip. You go from a decently smooth, open road to bumps that literally lift you off your seat. I had to take some anti-nausea medicine very early on. At one point, Zyan got pale and said her belly hurt. We thought she was going to be sick. Thankfully, we moved her up a few seats and cranked the AC. She did fall asleep and woke feeling better.

Our driver loved using his horn. Half the time, there was seemingly no reason. Along the trip, we saw it all. There was a ton of construction, some lush green land, dirt so thick the sky was foggy, people going to the restroom in the open, and so much more. Not only that, but a tire from a vehicle in front of us blew, and part of it hit our window. When we asked for prayers for safe travels, the need for answered prayer felt pressing. We also stopped at one rest stop. It was nothing like home. It consisted of open-air shops with food my stomach would never agree with, and you have to pay to use the restroom. That was a first for me. After six-plus hours of driving and searching for the correct building, our first stop was the Department of Social Welfare (DSW) in Kumasi. We needed to grab the letter that granted us permission to go to the orphanage and meet Bismark.

Much to our surprise, even though we were given verbal permission to go to the orphanage, the physical letter we needed wasn't ready when we arrived around 11:15 am. We had anticipated that this would be a quick stop to just grab the letter and go. Upon discovering that the letter still needed drafting, I knew we were going to be there for a long time. After our social worker and I explained the reason we were there, they assured us it wouldn't be long—as they returned to attend to some customers. All of the offices were just little rooms with open windows, and we sat in an outdoor hallway. I informed Spencer that we would be there for a while, so he brought the kids up to join us on some benches instead of standing downstairs outside the building waiting. The kids had been troopers all day. However, they were tired. Eventually, Liam had a meltdown. They could hear him from the office and instantly came out to us to see why he was crying. From our experience and from the education of those we came to know, culturally, crying wasn't well tolerated and made people uncomfortable. That show of emotion was not often displayed. A lady even grabbed him and tried standing him up and said, 'Oh, stop crying.' Guess what happened next? The customers who were in the office at the time were immediately done, and we were ushered in. I don't think I have ever felt thankful for a kid throwing a fit like I did in that moment.

Five people sat in that tiny office. They all questioned why Liam was crying and then got to business. It felt as if they hadn't done this before. We knew the office had conducted this business before, but we didn't know whether or not they were the same people. They asked odd questions and made us write down our address in the States, which was completely irrelevant to the reason we were there. We thought they might not even give us the letter. The guy in charge said that we couldn't take Bismark back home with us on that particular day after meeting him because we needed to give him a chance to warm up and 'feel lucky.' We originally expected not taking Bismark back with us that first day. However, we were told the day before that we could take him home on day one. We knew things could change, so it was okay. The guy typed the letter and sent us on our way after being at the DSW for about an hour and a half: next stop, the orphanage.

The trip to the orphanage after the DSW was also one I won't forget. Wow. They have a huge open-air market in Kumasi, the largest in Western Africa. It's impossible to explain fully, but I'll try my best. Imagine New Year's Eve, Times Square. Imagine everyone in attendance buying and selling things. Also, imagine the streets being open to traffic as well. The streets were being used by people more than cars. So, our trip was anything but quick. Everywhere you looked, people were buying, bargaining, organizing, selling, talking, eating, and even napping. These markets are the main way for locals to do their shopping for everyday items. People set up and tear down their shops on a daily basis. You can find luggage, jewelry, fresh fruits, vegetables, meat, kitchenware, clothes, shoes, fresh drinks, and so much more. It was an amazing sight to see.

Upon arriving at the Catholic-run orphanage around 1:30 pm, we pulled up, and some gates opened for our van to pull in. We got out of the van and sat on some benches outside under a small roof. That was the moment we had been waiting for, and we weren't completely sure what to expect. The orphanage workers said they would bring Bismark out to us soon. And they did. We remained seated on the benches as they walked him out to us. He was wearing the cutest jeans with buckles all over and a striped polo shirt. The workers had to wake him up from his nap when we got there, so he was pretty stoic at first. We introduced ourselves as 'mama' and 'daddy.' He looked at us, seemingly oblivious to what was happening. However, we gave each of our other three kids a little toy car to give to Bismark. That helped him warm up more quickly and opened the channels of comfortability. Eventually, we got half smiles…then full smiles…then some giggles. Bismark and the workers showed us around the orphanage. We saw his bed and the room he slept in. We saw the room with kids who had disabilities, the toddler room, and the baby room. You could see that the heat of the day and lack of truly nurturing care brought exhaustion upon everyone. The kids were either asleep (without blankets) or sat stoically, watching us explore. Man, it was a sight to see. I just wanted to scoop them all up and love on them.

We only got an hour with Bismark on that first day, but he warmed up well. He never really said anything. The girls loved him and kept grabbing his hands to usher him around. It was so sweet. And Nyla couldn't stop rubbing his hair. Liam liked him, but he was pretty indifferent. He and Liam were almost the same size, but Bismark was solid! For potentially not being well-fed, he was a good-sized kiddo. The workers had informed us that he was a good eater. When we had to leave for the day, Bismark wanted to come with us. We had noticed him looking at our van throughout our visit. He was hesitant to follow the workers when the time came.

After leaving, we got a call about one minute down the road saying that he was really crying. He was so sad he couldn't leave with us. It was hard to hear, but it made us happy that he wasn't scared and felt comfortable enough to go with us after such a short time.

We left and traveled to our apartment for the evening. A local missionary family graciously offered up an apartment they used to house people as needed. The complex was gated with locks and had barbed wire at the top of the apartments. Then, to get inside the apartment, you had to unlock another gate. That tells you how dangerous some areas of Kumasi are. The apartment was pretty rural, and the houses on that road were unbelievable. I literally didn't think some of the buildings could be houses because of the village-like feel and the one-room open buildings. The missionary hosting us said thieves used to break into the third-floor apartments where we were staying until they barred the windows. We were also informed not to go out at night. Kumasi is a big city, and it is more dangerous than Accra.

When we got to the apartment, we were hungry. We hadn't eaten a meal yet because of our busy schedule that day. The missionary drove Spencer and my dad to KFC for food, and we finally ate around 6 pm. The kiddos didn't love it as the KFC in Ghana is spicier than what we tend to eat. Food was limited, so thankfully, we packed oatmeal and snacks to curb the hunger. Cell service was equally as limited. All of Kumasi was pretty much a total dead zone for us. That was stressful because we couldn't use our apps to call for a driver, contact our social worker, order food, use our GPS, book anything for the next day, etc. Thank goodness our host gave us his Ghanaian phone so we could access a few things we needed.

We were hopeful and expectant that the next day, we would be able to take Bismark home with us. Had it been up to the workers at the orphanage, we would have been able to take him that first day.

After the stress of the drive to Kumasi, we decided to consider flying back home. We had to weigh the pros and cons of the price difference, safety, car sickness, Bismark's possible intolerance of cars/planes, time, and the availability of flights dependent on when we would arrive at the airport. We ultimately decided that flying would be our best option and booked flights for the next evening.

The resilience of the kids was amazing. After their long travel to Ghana, they endured an incredibly long, exhausting day just a few days later. They handled it like champs, and we heard very few complaints. However, everyone was ready for sleep at bedtime. The apartment didn't have AC, but the fans did work wonders, thankfully. Wouldn't you know it, at 12:30 am, our power went out. Apparently, that can happen randomly and usually lasts 4-5 hours at a time. I went straight to prayer after stressing for a moment. I was so far out of my comfort zone, and this was my first taste of what life in Ghana was like for the locals. I prayed that the power would come back on quickly, and the Lord answered with the power coming back on after about twenty minutes. We all desperately needed sleep that the power outage would certainly disturb." (End Journal Entry)

December 13, 2023

"Well, we got to go see Bismark again and then bring him home with us! Nyla and Zyan joined us as they desired, and we thought it would be great for them to see more kids and more of the orphanage. Yesterday, the older kids were all in school when we arrived, and the younger kids were napping, so we didn't see many of them. We got there at 8:45 am and just hung out and interacted with the kids who had disabilities until a sister brought Bismark out to us. As he approached, he was wearing the dearest jeans with a belt and yellow polo, and we saw him holding the three cars from the day before. We were able to play and interact with him and some of the other kids. The kids were all vying to have the cars that Bismark was holding. It was apparent that toys were a precious commodity and likely scarce at the orphanage. One sister gave two of Bismark's cars to other kids, which he was obviously sad about. But you bet he got them back before we left. He was determined not to leave without his new toys. As we played with Bismark, they brought the toddlers outside as well. Oh my goodness, my heart was in a puddle. The kids flocked to us, wanting to be held and loved. So, we did just that! Zyan jumped in on holding the kids, and even Nyla tried, though she wasn't much bigger than some of them. Those kids were starving for attention, which is a heartbreaking reality for kids in institutions all over the world.

We then requested to see Bismark's school before leaving. The school was about a five-minute walk from the orphanage. He was actually reluctant to walk with us, and we inferred that he thought we were taking him to school and leaving him there. We got to see Bismark's classroom, classmates, and teacher. We got pictures with everyone for him to have as he gets older. The sight of leaving the school is ingrained in my mind forever. As we left the school, dozens and dozens of school kids ran

105

outside their classrooms singing and chanting 'Obroni,' which means 'white man,' or more literally 'peeled one.'

After returning from the school and signing some papers, we got to bring Bismark back to the apartment with us. Watching him stare out the window and take everything in was truly a joy to my heart. He didn't say much, but he did say 'car' and was mesmerized by everything. Our taxi dropped us off at our apartment so we could settle Bismark into the family with gifts and things to call his own. He came to us with nothing but the clothes on his back (which I will keep forever). We had brought him a bookbag, headphones, a book with English words and pictures, a blanket, a water bottle, and a stuffed dinosaur (that he didn't like). We had some more cars for him as well as new clothes and shoes. He particularly enjoyed the book and showing off his skills to us. When we received Bismark's file back in the spring, we were informed that he didn't know English but rather the local language, Twi. Much to our surprise, as he looked at the picture book, he knew a lot of English words as he was learning them in school. The first picture he pointed out was 'key.' He had the sweetest accent, and how he said 'elephant' stole my heart. That moment on the bed in that apartment with Bismark telling us the names of pictures he saw is also one I will never forget.

The complex we were staying in had a trampoline in the common area, so we took the kids outside to let them jump. Bismark was hesitant and held on to Zyan the whole time. He quickly wanted down, so we took him in for a shower. They said that he was able to shower at the orphanage, so we thought he would jump right in. He didn't do that but rather stood towards the outside and let me wash him down with a cloth. While we knew he had more English than we originally thought, we weren't sure how much of what we were saying was being understood. We actually asked the missionary hosting us how to ask if he needed to use the restroom. She informed us that all the kids in that area simply said 'wee.' As impolite as it sounded, we would ask Bismark if he had to 'wee' to determine his level of potty training. Thankfully, he was completely potty-trained (except at nighttime). We did have to show him the workings of the toilet, though, as we were unsure what his bathroom commodities looked like at the orphanage.

After settling in, we had lunch. The missionary brought some local food that Bismark would like. We were so thankful for that because we didn't have much. Not only that, he was used to eating a more limited diet, so he couldn't go straight to an American diet at risk of getting sick. That, on top of the fact that he would possibly literally eat himself sick after not getting enough the past four years. We were told to stick to what he knows and then give him just a little bit of what we eat. We learned quickly what the caretaker at the orphanage meant when she said he was a good eater. We started with 'sausages,' which were chicken hot dogs. We had to cut him off after four and a half sausages. We also gave him some bread. He didn't like that. When he put it in his mouth, it got stuck to the roof, and he promptly pulled it out and refused to eat another slice. Many times, after lunch, he said, 'Sausage more.' But we knew we had to take it easy and wait before we fed him more. Honestly, watching him eat was pretty mesmerizing for the entire family.

We were informed that Bismark took naps at the orphanage, so we tried to lay him down for a nap. We didn't have much luck. He wouldn't stay in bed and started crying at one point, which broke my heart. Can you imagine what he could have been feeling? He was in a new environment, surrounded by total strangers guiding him. And honestly, we were clueless in this phase of parenting as well. We were trying to figure out what would be best for a little person we did not know yet. So, we just played some more. Bismark found the tablets we had brought with us and was fascinated. The other three kids got annoyed with him rather quickly when trying to watch something because he didn't care to watch anything. He just wanted to touch the screen. This was a whole new idea to him, and I am sure the cartoons were of little interest to his brain adjusting to television screens in a language he wasn't proficient in.

For dinner, Bismark had more sausages. He ate three this time. We tried to give him some crackers, but he didn't enjoy those either. We also gave him some 'biscuits,' which were similar to cookies but less sweet. He also didn't like those. He did snack on a few animal crackers. Later, he saw me drinking Coke, so I let him have a tiny sip. His reaction was too funny to ever forget. He was all smiles. Next thing we knew, he had found the larger bottle of Coke. We looked over and saw him holding it proudly as he wanted more 'black' to drink.

Then, we started our venture to the airport. The Kumasi airport was so different than any airport I had ever experienced. It was one tiny terminal. They had a waiting room in a building across the street if you arrived early for your flight. We sat at the only tiny restaurant they had and ordered chicken, rice, and french fries. Bismark LOVED the rice with chicken. He sat on my dad's lap and used his fingers to pick out and eat all the bits of chicken he could. He also picked out every piece of vegetable in the bowl to throw away. Sometimes, he used his fingers to eat the rice. He ate and ate. After that, we went to sit and wait. That was a bit tricky. Bismark was both curious and likely testing the waters to see what he could get away with. You could see on his face that he was ornery. We took turns following him around, holding him, and entertaining him. Every time he saw a television, he would point and say 'tv.' He was definitely fascinated with them. At one point in time, I asked, 'What is Bismark chewing on?' Much to my surprise, it was gum. We didn't give him gum. He had found it somewhere in the airport. I was mortified and took it from his mouth immediately. *Elf*, anyone?

When it was time for our flight, Bismark was excited about the airplane. The first time he heard a plane take off, I wish you could have seen his face. We walked back to the main building and went through security. They let us take the water onto the plane that we had brought from home, which was crazy to me. When it was time to board, we had to walk outside a bit to the airplane. Bismark's excitement and fascination turned to tears. He was tired and scared. The plane was a nice and exciting idea from afar, but getting on it was surely intimidating. Fortunately, he fell asleep on me right away on the plane. They let him sit on my lap the entire time. The way they accommodated us would not have happened on the big flights we had previously done, so I was thankful that this was his first experience.

Bedtime that first night was so difficult. Bismark knew that he could just get out of bed, so he did—a lot. We consistently took him back in and laid him down. We tried a pack-n-play, but he just climbed right out. When we tried laying him down in bed, he cried. It was so hard because he was crying and saying something, but we didn't know what. I just can't imagine what his little mind was thinking and the big feelings he must have been feeling. We eventually got him to sleep by lying in bed with him after he was super exhausted." (End Journal Entry)

The experience we had at the orphanage was eye-opening. People often ask if we think that the kids were well taken care of and loved. While I think that the basic needs of the kids were being met, there were many other needs not being met. The ratio of the number of workers to the children was overwhelming. In many ways, I do think the workers do the best they can with what they are given. However, the children greatly lacked love and connection. We witnessed a kid fall down and scrape his head, which resulted in bleeding. Instead of being embraced and cared for as he cried, one of the sisters pointed and said something along the lines of "See, he fell down." There simply were not enough caretakers to meet the demands of the job and ensure the kids were shown empathy and love. We witnessed a heart-breaking interaction between Bismark and one of the sisters in which he was threatened that he would not go home with us based on his performance, or lack thereof. What we witnessed makes my heart ache for what we may not be seeing. I ache for the children who are told they may never have parents because their behavior isn't worthy. I ache for the kids who see other kids like Bismark leaving the orphanage with a family. I ache for the kids who question why nobody loves them and why they were abandoned. I ache for the kids running to us with lifted arms, begging to be loved. I choose to remember and mourn for the life that these kids are growing up in. I choose to pray that the orphan crisis will one day come to an end.

The orphan crisis is real and heartbreaking, and I am so thankful for the small role that God directed us to in order to care for "one of the least of these." (Matthew 25:40) I remember the first time I saw Bismark; I noticed that his front left tooth had the cutest little chip in it. His eyelashes were beautiful and curled up above his deep brown eyes. He had the sweetest line at the base of his nose. Those first days with Bismark were days of growth, learning, and blessing. Welcoming him into our hearts and homes was a gift from the Lord.

We were able to see the goodness of God's perfect timing in everything as we reflected upon our time in Kumasi. If we had gotten the letters we needed and were able to travel when we first arrived in Ghana, we would have had our desires met by not having our kids with us at the orphanage. However, the Lord knew that having them with us would be so much sweeter than we could have imagined. The kids were able to naturally connect with Bismark in a way that Spencer and I couldn't. There was a greater sense of ease as we transitioned him into our lives because of the connection through play and childlike innocence. It was also a beautiful blessing to see our biological children interact with kids at the orphanage and school. They loved on and embraced them in what I believe was a life-changing experience.

I find myself thanking God for the faithfulness of His timing in regard to this situation. We obviously couldn't have planned it better ourselves. God always has a plan when we go through challenging circumstances (and waiting for the letter through those initial days was tough). It doesn't mean that bad things aren't bad. They are. Sin is a reality in the fallen world we live in. However, good can come from the bad. Romans 8:28 says, "And we know that for those who love God all things work together for good, for those who are called according to his purpose."

One thing that I have learned is to wait on the Lord. The Lord brought good from our hard circumstances, but it took time. Psalm 27:14 says, "Wait for the Lord; be strong, and let your heart take courage; wait for the Lord!" Waiting is not easy, but we can lean into the Lord to provide us with everything we need to endure the wait. During those weeks of waiting for the letter, we were presented with the option to fly back home more than once. That option was devastating and offensive. We had come too far to turn around and go back home. I am sure that is exactly what Satan would have had us do and possibly miss out on one of the biggest blessings of our lives. Thankfully, we waited on the Lord to bring good from our bad to meet our Kwadwo "Bismark" alongside our other children.

Challenge/Question for Thought: What do you need to wait on the Lord for? What "bad" are you experiencing that you can allow God to bring "good" to?

CHAPTER 10

The Making of a Name

Names. Some carry familial significance. Others carry the weight of meaning found in the word. Others still are given due to the beauty they inspire in the parents giving the name. Names are important as they identify who we are to other people. Especially biblically, names carried weight and value. In the New Testament, we see Saul's name changed to Paul after he converted to following Jesus. As Saul, he was killing Christians. But as Paul, he was following the name of Christ and making Him known. That name change is an example of a new direction in Paul's life. Another example we read says, "She will bear a son, and you shall call his name Jesus, for he will save his people from their sins." (Matthew 1:21) That verse is an example of a name bearing prophetic weight.

In Matthew 1:23, we read, "'Behold, the virgin shall conceive and bear a son, and they shall call his name Immanuel' (which means God with us)." This name for Jesus is a description of how God became man to dwell with humans on earth. There are a plethora of names used for God throughout the Bible that reflect His very nature and character. A few examples are El Roi (the God who sees), Adonai (Lord), El Shaddai (God Almighty), and Jehovah Jireh (the Lord our provider).

Throughout the process of adoption, a common question we received from people was, "Will you change your child's name?" Now, there was not a straightforward answer in which I could give a definitive "yes" or "no." Many factors played into determining the name of our future child. First of all, it would depend on how old the child would be when we adopted them. For example, if the child was called a specific name for four or five years, we may not want to change it as enough of their life would already be thrown into shifting waters. That would have been their identity for so many years that

119

changing it may be more harmful than helpful. Secondly, the complexity of the name was also important. Other countries often choose names that are culturally appropriate using their own dialects and significance. If the name were one that others would fail miserably at pronouncing in our culture, we may have considered changing it. Of course, it wouldn't really matter if people messed it up— because we mess up names that are given within our culture all the time. Lastly, as mentioned above, names can carry a lot of weight, cultural significance, and identity. The possibility of taking that important piece from our child based on our preference was never our heart's desire. But again, we wanted to figure out the given name first in order to make that decision. Basically, we were holding onto the idea of naming, or not naming, our child loosely.

You may have noticed in the beginning that I mentioned we were paired up with a little boy named Kwadwo Bismark in May of 2023. It is true; that was his name originally. We were told that the nuns at the orphanage gave him that name. Names often have a particular cultural importance in Ghana, even more so than names in America. People are given names based on family, prophetic meaning, days of the week, etc. From our experience, I would say that most names are given with great care and significance. In Ghana, many people are named after a day in the week, depending on the tribe they are from. There are male and female day names for each day of the week.

Our son's day name happened to be Kwadwo, pronounced *Quajoe*, as the "dw" in the local dialect takes on the "j" sound of our alphabet. Kwadwo is the name of a male born on Monday in Ghana. Bismark was the name given to him that he was often referred to at the orphanage. So, the original birth certificate that we received had Kwadwo as his first name and Bismark as his last name (we don't know his familial last name). Within Ghanaian culture, Bismark means "a person who is carrying a good news. Or someone who often speaks words of encouragement and comfort and peace and salvation and redemption from God."

We went back and forth as to how we wanted Bismark's name to read on his birth certificate, as we already knew he would still be called Bismark. We never questioned changing that aspect of his name. I asked for opinions from family and specifically asked the locals what was most culturally relevant. I took into account his future and the ease of conducting business if his legal name did, or did not, match the name he would be called. I also sought out the Lord in prayer. I did not want to make that decision haphazardly or flippantly. We ultimately decided that we would simply flip-flop the order and call him Bismark Kwadwo Draper when we legally became his parents and made that change in court.

Honestly, I couldn't have come up with a more beautiful or culturally significant name myself. The Lord knew Bismark's life would be an example to me and others that adoption is a reflection of a believer's life in Christ. Not only that, but my prayer is that our Bismark accepts the Lord as his Savior and carries the good news of salvation with him to share with others for the rest of his life. His name is also a beautiful reminder of the Lord's goodness over my life, specifically in the area of adoption. While carrying significant weight and meaning as a reflection of salvation, we also got to keep the cultural importance of his name as the middle name.

There is so much of Bismark's story that I would love to share with the world. However, when Bismark is old enough, I want him to share his story as he sees fit. For those curious, I will simply share how Bismark got to the orphanage. He was brought into the orphanage around the age of two by a lady who saw the need for a little boy to receive proper care. When we first received Bismark's profile in May, the phone number of that specific lady was listed in his social welfare report. While in Ghana, I remembered that the name and number had been given to us inadvertently and decided to seek the lady out, prayerful that her number had not changed. By God's provision, I reached out, and she responded. I was actually able to meet the lady who saved Bismark's life while in Kumasi on a second trip to complete the court processes. We got some beautiful pictures of him with his "grandma" that I will allow him to share someday. She was elated and emotional and said, "I love you" to me and him multiple times. Truly, Bismark's name is a testament to his life and the work that God did to bring him into our family.

While I love the names given to all of our children, I pray that, ultimately, they will bear the name of Christ. 2 Corinthians 5:17 says, "Therefore, if anyone is in Christ, he is a new creation. The old has passed away; behold the new has come." We are often taught that who we are is entirely new when we accept Christ as our Savior and choose to follow Him. That is absolutely true. Because of the work of Christ on the cross, we are presented to the Father as holy and blameless, as stated in Colossians 1:22: "He has now reconciled in his body of flesh by his death, in order to present you holy and blameless and above reproach before him." In the same way, we are also given a new name. We have a right to be called children of God. John 1:12 says, "But to all who did receive him, who believed in his name, he gave the right to become children of God." Our earthly names may or may not carry great meaning, but finding a new identity in Christ is of the utmost significance.

You see, we often allow the world to create or tarnish our identity. We find identity in our jobs, social circles, leisurely enjoyment, etc. We find our identity in the sports we enjoy, the instruments we play, or the friendships we create. Those are not bad things. However, the issue is when we place our identity in them, we can "lose" our identity when things get difficult. Maybe a friend turned on you and left you feeling unworthy to be loved in friendship. Maybe you lost a job you loved, so you feel like you aren't valuable to employers and will never flourish in the workplace. Maybe you became injured, and your inability to play a sport you excelled in leaves you feeling like you now live a life without purpose. By misplacing identity, it is easy to believe the lies that come in those areas of life when things don't work out.

In my life, I can say that I found a lot of value and identity in my health in relation to my ability to work out. Early on in my marriage with Spencer, I fell in love with working out in order to be a healthier version of myself. Working out is a wonderful thing. I truly believe that we need to be healthy temples so as to serve God and serve others well. Here is the issue. I can't work out at all in this season of my life. I am physically unable to work out like I once did. That piece of identity (good health allowing me to work out and, therefore, creating good health) for me has been stripped away. For so long, I have beat myself up over my inability to do what I once loved. I pray that I can get back to where I was someday, but the Lord has taught me a great lesson through the challenge of what was taken from me. My identity is in Christ alone and not in the health of my body.

I could give you so many examples of how I put my identity in all of the wrong places and how that did not fare well in my life. What I now know is that when we place our identity in Christ and take on a new name, the world has no jurisdiction to give or take away our worth. We can declare freedom through the power of the Spirit who lives inside of us to identify with Christ in every aspect of our lives. There is a song by Josh Baldwin that starts, "I know who I am 'cause I know who You are." When we remember who God is and how He gives us a new identity in Christ, we can remember who we are—children of God.

I am so thankful for the name God gave Bismark—which is a blessing and reminder in my life to place my identity in the One who carries the best news that the world so desperately seeks to find. If it weren't for the miraculous working of the Lord's sovereignty, I would never have known the name "Bismark" in a beautiful and refining way in my life, as continually revealed throughout the adoption process and thereafter.

Challenge/Question for Thought: Have you ever contemplated your name as a child of God, or do you put more importance on the earthly name given to you? In what areas of your life have you misplaced or allowed the world to define your identity?

CHAPTER 11

Officially a Draper

Our time in Ghana was filled with a lot of really great moments and a lot of really hard moments. I would love to clue you into a bit of what life in Ghana looked like for us, as I know many people love to hear about the experiences of others. First of all, it was hot… stifling hot. The temperature was about 85 degrees, with a real feel of 100 degrees every single day. We happened to be in Ghana during the dry season, which meant we didn't see much rain or much relief in temperature. Every day was pretty predictable in that regard. Initially, we walked a lot, but then we used Bolt (like Uber) for all transportation to destinations further away. Fortunately, we could walk to most places we needed. However, it wasn't easy carrying bags of groceries, keeping an eye on four children walking home from the store on busy roads with no sidewalks, and sweat dripping down every inch of our bodies.

When we arrived in Ghana, we met another adoptive family who had been there for TWO years for their adoption. Because of them, we met a man who became our personal driver. Having a driver was invaluable. We didn't have to rely on the availability of a Bolt driver. We didn't have to stand around waiting for someone to show up. We didn't have to stress when we were in areas with little to no cell service. The only downfall was that our driver did not have working air conditioning in his car. I spent many hours and days sitting in that car, sweating. They say it builds character, right? Our driver, Jeffrey, was a blessing in so many ways. He would show up in the morning when we needed him to and take us anywhere and everywhere. He went above and beyond by carrying in sleeping children or heaps of groceries. He was our bargain guy when we went to local markets and were overcharged for items. Jeffrey loved the Lord and encouraged me in my faith more times than I can count. When my entire family returned to America, He helped me in situations I couldn't have endured alone.

When we went to Ghana, we knew that Spencer had a limited amount of FMLA time. The plan was for him to be there with me and the kids for two months. A lot happened in those first months. We met our son and spent one month doing a required bonding time. In that month, my dad spent three weeks with us, while my mom spent four weeks with us. We traveled north to Tamale, Ghana, and went on a two-day safari at Mole National Park. That was the experience of a lifetime. We spent evenings taking turns trying to get Bismark to go to sleep. We took many trips down to the apartment pool to spend hours in the water. We went to a movie theater in Ghana, which was a unique experience in many ways. We also celebrated our first Christmas as a family of six. That day was extremely difficult for me as I have never spent Christmas away from home. I was also dreading

New Year's Eve. Just as it rolled around, new friends we met from the States reached out to us and invited us to their home to celebrate. It was a blessing to connect with them and then continue to build that friendship over my time in Ghana. We spent time preparing for the next steps and working through what that may look like. We spent time helping homeschool the kids and then enrolling them in a nearby Montessori school that they attended three days a week. Indeed, our time was full of memories.

At the beginning of February 2024, Spencer had to leave Ghana to return home to work. Spencer and I would be away from each other for an indefinite amount of time (and surely longer than we had originally planned due to the new four-month timeframe). The blessing of the timing was after Spencer left for the States, his parents joined me and the kids for two weeks. The thought of raising four kids alone in a foreign country was intimidating, to say the least. After they left, I was on my own for the next week…kind of. We had an amazing house-help who had become a friend. Again, we met her through the same adoptive family I mentioned. She did all of our cooking, cleaning, and laundry. She would babysit when needed, grocery shop at local markets, pick up kids from school, and so much more.

We had a three-bedroom apartment, so once all the parents left, we had an empty bedroom. Contrary to what we had planned, the boys slept in my room every night, and the girls slept in the other bedroom together. Our helper, Asana, was gracious enough to live with the kids and me in the absence of the whole family. I think we were both equally blessed by that time. Asana made our beds, cleaned sheets way too often when a kid had an accident, washed out lunch boxes, and cleaned shoes. She went above and beyond to make our time much more comfortable and enjoyable. Throughout many stages of the process, she was an emotional support and cultural sounding board. After that initial week of just me and the kids, my dad returned to Ghana again. While he was there, I fell pretty sick, and then Liam came down with a similar illness. We were a mess. On a Sunday morning, when Asana didn't normally work, she came to the rescue to pick up the slack that I couldn't manage. One time, when I was really sick, she even took my stool sample via an ordered Bolt to a local doctor to have it tested. Now that is true love—and also the convenience of life in Ghana.

The relationships and connections made in Ghana were beautiful. I met two pharmacists who cared so deeply when I was ill. I had built a relationship with them over time as I went to that same pharmacy any time there was a need. In Ghana, we didn't need a prescription to get most medications. We could walk into a pharmacy, tell them what was wrong, and they would give us the necessary medication. That was a major convenience because we could access everything we needed (and more) without having to see a doctor. Relationships were of critical importance in all aspects of life in Ghana. You know the saying, "it's not what you know, it's who you know?" Well, it

134

rang loud and true in Ghana. Having connections was the best way to get things done.

We lived in a lovely apartment that was very European-like. It was simple and practical. Each room had its own wall air conditioning unit, which was super convenient. We had worked into our contract that the services (AC, internet, etc.) would be included in the rent price. What we didn't know was that those services had caps. We found that out the hard way when our electricity was no longer working after arriving home one evening. We had to "top up" our electricity whenever it was getting low in order to continue to have services. We like to live in comfort, so we certainly used the AC liberally, not knowing there was a limit. This was the common practice in Ghana, though. You would have to load money onto an account to prepay for services. Having worked it into our contract actually complicated things because none of the workers really understood that we shouldn't have had to pay for more services, as is customary. We learned that it was also common for the government to issue "lights out" in certain areas at certain times. Thankfully for us, our apartment had a generator so as not to be affected by that. We did have times when only part of our electricity worked in random locations in the apartment. It did not affect the air conditioning, but it did impact the water heater. We had to deal with that ongoing breaker/wiring issue for some time.

Our apartment had 24/7 security, which basically just meant a guard sat at a gate, unarmed, and opened it to let people in and out. We had no idea the role of security prior to arriving. We lived in a very safe area that never left us feeling uneasy. We learned that most crimes were crimes of opportunity. That meant that simply having a guard at the entrance deterred people from attempting any sort of criminal activity. We could walk to a few restaurants, pharmacies, stores, several embassies, and other amenities; yet, we lived rural enough that it wasn't loud or busy. Across the street from the apartment entrance was a little "market" that was set up daily. We often bought our bottled water from them for the ease of carrying it back to the apartment. We had to drink bottled water our entire time in Ghana, as you may have suspected.

Most days were simple. We spent time doing school work, swimming, watching movies, and relaxing. There was not a lot to do. After staying for a week in the country, my dad left and took the girls along with him, but not before attending court. The girls were ready to go home after having been there for nearly three months. Every goodbye they had to say when family left Ghana was heartbreaking. They would lose all control, and people would check on us to ensure everything was alright. It was hard for me to say goodbye to the girls, as I had never left them for more than six days, just one time the year prior. However, I knew that it would be best. Once my dad left, it would be me and the boys for the foreseeable future. At that point, we had stayed in Ghana for about three months, which you may remember was only a month shy of the time we were told to anticipate being there altogether. However, we had no idea when we would actually be going home, as we still had many steps to go through before completing the process.

The in-country process was straightforward on paper but not in practicality. We were required to spend one month bonding with Bismark starting the day we brought him back home with us. That was a pretty peaceful month in the sense that we had nothing that needed to get done. Therefore, we could enjoy the time without the pressure of deadlines. All of the holidays fell within that month, which I mentioned, Ghanaians celebrate big. Not much business would have happened within that timeframe, anyway. After that bonding period, we needed a social worker to come to our apartment and write a report for us to be sent in a file for court. That took several weeks to complete, from the visit to having the report sent to the courthouse. After that, we had to wait for court. Initially, we thought the court hearing might happen while Spencer was still in Ghana, which would have been our ideal. Once we realized that timeline would not be met, we were hoping that it would fall within the timeframe of Spencer's parents being in town to help with the kids as I traveled with Bismark to Kumasi. As time passed, we continued waiting for a court date, and we realized that was not going to happen either. Waiting for a court date was painful. We received a proposed court date and quickly learned it was just that... proposed. That date changed over and over again, getting pushed back for reasons unbeknownst to us. I spent many nights calling Spencer and crying in frustration at the situation.

Thankfully for me, but maybe not my dad, the court hearing took place during his one-week stay in Ghana. He had the job of taking care of and keeping three kids alive and entertained while I made the trip back to Kumasi with Bismark. Asana also joined me on that trip, for which I am so incredibly thankful. I could not have done that day without her. In fact, that day was one that I would love to recount for you because the power of God was so clearly evident in our lives.

Our projected court date changed and was pushed back countless times, as mentioned above. The day before the next projected court date of February 27, we waited all day to figure out what was going on and if that date would be changed again. We had been in limbo for nearly a month but did not see a reason why the date would change again. We had booked flights for 7 pm to go to Kumasi on Monday, February 26. Through an email that I received that very Monday afternoon, we were told that our case had not been filed in court yet and that they would move the case to the next available court date of March 5th. We were devastated that the date was being moved yet again. But even more than that, the 6th is their Independence Day, so we weren't hopeful that date would stick either. As soon as I received that email, I was crushed. I called our adoption agency to have a conversation immediately and then called Spencer to fill him in and express my anger and sadness. Our adoption agency and the Ghana lawyers representing us all had an impromptu meeting after we were given that most recent update. After that meeting, we were advised to go to Kumasi as scheduled and show up at court the next day because we had been given misinformation, and our case had apparently been filed. We also knew that we would have an advocate when we arrived who would plead with the judge on our behalf in court.

So, Bismark, Asana, and I hopped in the car with packed bags to catch our flight. On our way to the airport (only a ten-minute drive from our apartment), I got a text saying that our case was NOT actually filed in court as we were recently informed and that it would be filed the next morning. They informed us that the judge may or may not be willing to see us. The judge wouldn't have had adequate time to review our case that same day if filed in the morning. If we were to be seen at all the next day, it would likely be in the afternoon instead of the morning as planned. Not only was our situation specifically up in the air but we were informed by our agency and other adoptive families that it was very common for the court date to be changed upon

141

arriving the day of court. It was typically only by a day or two, but that was when the judge HAD adequate time to review the file. We understood that going to Kumasi was a risk at that point, given the circumstances. Our adoption agency left that decision up to us as they had no control over the outcome of the situation. There was no guarantee the judge would see us, but there was also no guarantee that they wouldn't. I distinctly remember hearing from the Lord and receiving the prompting that going to Kumasi was the correct decision. We went ahead and decided to continue to the airport and show up in court the next day.

That decision began a journey of witnessing miracles...but not without first experiencing corruption and opposition. On the way to the airport, we got pulled over, my first time since being in Ghana. We had heard the stories about corrupt officials but hadn't experienced it firsthand. Jeffrey was driving, and I was in the passenger seat, with Bismark and Asana in the back. The officer pulled us over for not wearing seatbelts. Hardly anyone wears seat belts in Ghana, so we were surprised when that was the reason. The stories from my ex-pat friends who were pulled over relentlessly for money were unsettling. From our experience and the experiences of our friends, many of the police officers were quite corrupt. Of course, that wasn't across the board. One of my good friends I met in Ghana was a police officer herself. She was able to give us insight into how the system works, the desperation of locals to bring money home to the family, and the collaborative efforts of the officers to make that happen. The officer who pulled us over told us to cancel our trip after Jeffrey explained to him that we were headed to the airport to go to court for our adoption. The officer also said that Jeffrey's driver's license was expired and tried advising me on that. I can tell you that his license was NOT expired, but the officer was relentless with us. The next thing I knew, he got into the backseat of the car. As Jeffrey proceeded to the airport, the officer said, "Go to the police station." In that moment, my heart was in a bit of turmoil and filled with fear.

Within seconds, we cut to the chase and asked the officer what he wanted. A bit of negotiating took place, and he got more than is typical of those situations, but we were able to settle the affair and head on our way.

We had a great flight (Asana's first ever) to Kumasi. Upon landing, we took a Bolt to the hotel we had booked near the location of the courthouse. It was a cute little hotel with a great courtyard (where we met the lady who saved Bismark's life) and served breakfast in the morning. We woke up early the following day to head to court and pray for miracles. I will share with you my revised journal entry from the day of court because it was truly full of miracles. It was a day in which I could physically FEEL the prayers of hundreds of family members and friends back home. I am so thankful for that particular day because if it had never happened, I would have never known the Spirit's comfort and the tangible effects of prayer on the body. My mind carried a lot of weight surrounding our situation, but my body and spirit felt the prayers being sent up on

144

our behalf. It was unlike anything I could ever describe adequately, and it was beautiful. It was also a day in which 1 Thessalonians 5:17 became a more present reality in my life. That verse simply says, "pray without ceasing." Not only was prayer a beautiful reality of that day, but it was a convicting reality that I should pray without ceasing every day, not just on days in which I feel a pressing need for the Lord to show up. Because honestly…we do need the Lord to show up for us every day. When we pretend we don't or don't acknowledge that we need Him, we are believing in the false idea that we are in ultimate control. What would life look like if continual prayer was my heart's poster every single day…in the mundane or in the middle of a crisis?

February 27, 2024

"We got up early to eat breakfast before going to court at 8:40 am. We checked out of our hotel and, therefore, had our luggage with us all day. Prior to this day, I realized that no one had sent us the location of the courthouse, so we just showed up at a nearby courthouse I found on my phone. We sat in a waiting room at the entry while I tried to make some contacts to figure out what would happen next. Unsurprisingly, we were at the wrong courthouse. We got ahold of our advocate in Kumasi and were sent to the proper location and had a taxi take us there. On the way there, our lawyer called. She informed us that she had filed the application that morning. That was the first miracle, as we were told that our case would be filed a week ago and wasn't. We had no idea if it would be filed that morning, but it was. The lawyer said she had left the courthouse after filing our case and that we should return to the court to see the judge at 1:00 pm. That was the second miracle because many judges would not even consider seeing families if they didn't have time to review the application a day (or days) beforehand. Our judge may have not even seen the file prior to our ten-minute hearing later that day. Now, had we known that court would be in the afternoon just an hour earlier, we could have stayed at our hotel comfortably until noon.

Instead, a taxi took us to a nearby outdoor cafe. Thankfully, there was shade, but after spending three hours there, we were hot. We didn't have any other options, so we set up camp and made the best of the situation. I have never been so thankful for tablets and snacks. Those two things kept Bismark's busy body mostly content for such a long time. At 12:15 pm, we grabbed our luggage and walked to the courthouse to meet our lawyer at 12:30 pm. We were dragging suitcases, carrying Bismark, and sweating the entire way. It was a fairly short walk, but I am sure we were a sight to behold. I was dressed in a long, thick, nice dress to appear before a judge. Taxis kept trying to rescue us, and we got a lot of odd looks from strangers. We went to the courtroom that our contact told us to go to. We were dripping in sweat upon arrival, looking a bit disheveled. We got many looks in the courthouse, people questioned what we were doing, and a police officer even approached us with apprehension. Apparently, our contact had given us the wrong location, so we were then escorted down the stairs and down the outdoor hall to the correct courtroom. I briefly met the lawyer, and then we were told to sit and wait to be called back. Fortunately, we only sat there for about ten minutes because there was no AC, and Bismark's patience was running thin.

We were then quickly escorted into the judge's chambers. The experience in that room was cold and hostile. While I did not know exactly what to expect, I certainly couldn't have predicted what we experienced. We had a female judge who hardly acknowledged our entrance or even glanced our way. I walked in with Bismark, our lawyer, a social worker, and another lady. They told Bismark and me to sit on some couches that did not face the judge at all. We sat facing another couch, staring at a wall, while the three workers sat in front of the judge to our right. The next ten minutes felt like one million years. Bismark started crying slowly initially, but then it turned to full sobs. It is hard to know exactly what he was feeling as he didn't communicate anything, but I imagine he was scared (and certainly exhausted). We were in a new environment, and he had no idea what was going on. I am sure he also felt the tension the room and likely in my body. Eventually, I decided to stand and rock him, singing quietly as they continued on with business. I'll be honest: his crying made me nervous. I wondered if the judge thought the adoption wasn't a good fit. Or if she thought I handled his crying inappropriately. Or maybe, on the contrary, it helped as she saw me rock him because she saw my care for him. My mind was swirling with possible conjectures and how to handle the situation in a manner that would be deemed appropriate by the judge. I realized that it didn't matter because I couldn't control the situation. I simply prayed. I heard the lawyer explaining our case, why Spencer wasn't there, and how Bismark had three siblings and would have a better life with a family. I glanced over to try and see the judge once in a while. She didn't say much and seemed to be flipping through our file. At one point, I thought I heard the word 'granted,' but I couldn't be sure over the sobs. The judge read an official statement, followed by the lawyer reading an official statement. The next thing I knew, we were walking out of the courtroom. I looked around, unsure of what happened. I looked at our contact and asked, 'So, is it official?' One lady quietly said, 'yes.' It was absolutely anticlimactic for one of the most joyous occasions of our lives. The adoption was granted! That was the third miracle. All of the odds were against us. But we serve a God who is FOR us. Romans 8:31 says, 'What then shall we say to these things? *If God is for us, who can be against us?*' I am so thankful that I serve a God who trumps all earthly powers." (End Journal Entry)

My words simply cannot convey the power and presence of the Spirit on that particular day. One thing that I must also acknowledge was the supernatural strength that the Lord granted me. The Lord sustained me on that particular day and every other day while in Africa. My health was certainly a concern many times prior to traveling, but the Lord provided a supernatural tenacity that could not be done with my own will and power. Many days, and that one in particular, were full and exhausting. Life in Ghana was much harder than life in America. Simple tasks were anything but simple, and the heat was enough to exhaust anyone. However, I am so thankful for the ways in which the Lord showed up in Kumasi and the timing of His will in the days before and after court.

Challenge/Question for Thought: What would life look like if continual prayer was your heart's poster every single day? Where have you seen the supernatural or miracle-working power of the Lord in your life?

CHAPTER 12

Big Yellow House

The days following the court hearing were chalked full of unanticipated surprises that only the Lord could have known. Our court date was held on February 27, just over three months since being in the country. On March 2, my dad flew home with Zyan and Nyla after their nearly three-month stay. A new era of the adoption process was ushered in. I was going to finish the journey with the boys while Asana lived with us to care for and support us. We knew what needed to happen in order for me and the boys to make the journey back home. We also knew that the odds of hitting our initial four-month timeline were looking grim but not impossible. I was prayerfully desiring to be home with my family by Easter. What lie ahead of us in regard to the timing was one of the most stretching times of my life to this day.

We needed the judge to sign the court documents, we needed to receive another document called the court attestations, and we needed to apply for and retrieve Bismark's new birth certificate with his official new name. After receiving the birth certificate, we would apply for Bismark's passport and then visa. We learned that different parts of the process caused issues for different adoptive families. For us, that was the birth certificate. Once we received the court attestations after the judge's signature, we applied for the birth certificate. Even applying for it involved some hiccups. We wanted to hire our own person to file the application because we had information that they would be able to follow through with the process quickly for us. Unfortunately, our contact on the grounds in Ghana went ahead and filed the application on our behalf without first checking with us. We had to retract our initial application so as not to cause confusion when our application showed up twice in the system. To be completely honest, there was confusion and chaos surrounding the entire birth certificate process. I won't get into the nitty-gritty of it, but we went through weeks of back and forth, causing a lot of emotional turmoil for me. As mentioned before, I was alone for the last stretch of the journey, and it was humbling.

Mid-March, about a week after filing for the birth certificate, the unimaginable happened. All internet service was down. Initially, I did not think much about it, but I quickly learned that it was a much bigger deal than just losing internet for a day. We learned that an anchor from a boat at sea had actually cut an underwater cable, causing a massive outage in much of Africa. We had been stressed by the things that kept happening within the adoption process, but that blow hit the hardest. In fact, news outlets were saying it could take four weeks or more to restore service completely. The outage also affected my cell service. It was typical that my cell service was spotty, but when that happened, I didn't have hardly any phone capabilities. I was cut off from my family and friends. Thankfully, Asana was still able to use her phone, and she let me use it whenever I needed to. One evening, I nearly panicked over the situation. I remember calling Spencer as tears rolled down my face.

I was growing weary in the journey, so Spencer and I discussed the next steps. We knew that the internet issue would cause a delay in the birth certificate, as it affected nearly everything in Ghana. We were considering my possible return to the States, getting a foster for Bismark, and then returning to Ghana when things picked back up. That felt like a really hard option. Whenever a family member had left Ghana and Bismark got upset, I made sure to tell him, "Mama isn't leaving until you are." I wanted to assure him that he could trust us as his new family to form a healthy attachment. We had been telling him all about his new home, which was coined "big yellow house." We assured him that everyone who left went to the big yellow house and that he would soon go there as well. I was struggling with not staying true to my word and the trust that could be broken in a critical time of building trust. We reached out to another adoptive family who had to leave their child with a foster. They encouraged us that while it was an option that was incredibly hard, it could actually build trust when Bismark would see me come back for him. We also threw out the option of having the girls brought back to Ghana for a while. That option would be really expensive and one that would require us to look for new housing to make it more affordable. As it stood, we were renewing rent at the current apartment for two weeks at a time.

We discussed our options for some time while I stole away to a local internet café once in a while to reconnect with the world and get some work done. Somehow, the café had access to some alternative internet source in situations like the one I found myself. They were packed full of business with increased prices, but the convenience was well worth it to me when necessary. I went days without any connection, so the ability to simply reach out to people refreshed my soul.

Of course, God knew that the cable would be severed before we ever went to Ghana, but we could have never anticipated such a fluke in the process. Thankfully, the internet was restored much more quickly than we had anticipated, and we had full service in our area about one week later. We put a halt on coming up with options for what to do next, but we did decide that Spencer would come out for a short trip in April (after being apart for two months) and then take Liam back home. I loved having both boys and watching their relationship grow. They would play with each other for hours on end, which was beautiful to witness. However, we knew that it would be easiest for me to get Bismark home on my own if Spencer could get Liam home toward the end of the journey.

On Easter morning, Spencer showed up in Ghana for a quick trip together. Honestly, it was a refreshing time. Our marriage hadn't reached any state of healing while in Ghana...during our time together or apart. To be really vulnerable, I was ready for him to leave in February and enjoyed him not being there for two months. I was honest with Spencer about that. Even with the many counseling sessions we had, our marriage was nowhere near a state of glorifying God. But isn't it just like God to do miraculous things? I have to share a story that dates back nearly nine years.

In 2015, we went to California to watch Spencer walk for his college graduation. Upon attending, we knew that he still had one class to finish, but they allowed him to walk while withholding the diploma. While I do not regret getting married at such a young age and would not go back and change a thing, life had hit really hard while we were married and both in college. Spencer was working full-time (mandatory seven days a week) for much of that time. That, on top of a full college course load at a rigorous school, proved to be too much. When the time came for Spencer to finish his last semester of college, the senior project required more work than was manageable. Spencer decided that he would finish the final course at a later date.

The "later date" never happened. Honestly, I allowed it to cause some bitterness in my heart. Even though I knew it was too much to finish at the time, I was not extending grace in his decision not to finish his degree. He was getting a degree in biblical studies, which he no longer planned to use vocationally. Spencer had a great job at a factory that he enjoyed. I had brought up the degree once in a while with Spencer over the years until I eventually stopped mentioning it altogether. In my heart, it felt like all that time, money, and effort spent to ultimately drop out of the process felt like a waste. Fast forward to the summer of 2023. Spencer had the opportunity to take on a promotion at his job. He applied for the position that they offered him soon after. The requirement for the job, though? He had to have a bachelor's degree. It felt like an inconvenience because he actually had to take several more classes than just that senior project class he didn't finish. So, we paid the fee (thankfully, the college is super affordable), and he began classes in the fall of 2023 while working a new position and preparing for Africa. He was able to manage his time really well and work on school in ways that didn't negatively impact the family. I am sure it wasn't always easy, but Spencer worked hard and even brought the schoolwork to Ghana.

Spencer learned that one of the classes he had taken years ago no longer counted on his transcript, so he would have to choose a new elective to take in the spring of 2024 alongside his senior project class. He had two options and chose to take Marriage and Family Counseling. It sounded interesting and beneficial. And boy, was it beneficial. The timing of taking the additional class was perfect because while I was in Ghana with the kids, he returned home to the States and was able to pour himself into his job and schoolwork. But even more beneficial than the timing lining up was the content in which he had learned.

While in Ghana together, I felt like I was always tip-toeing around Spencer and did not fully enjoy being with him, which was why I felt content when he left. When I initially expressed that to Spencer, he acknowledged that his heart was not in a good place at all when he was in Ghana. He was now literally being transformed by the faithful words of the teacher who taught his elective class. He was excited to return to Ghana to spend time with me and try to repair what had been torn before. The miracle of God's timing in regard to Spencer's schooling was a beautiful example of how God truly works everything together for our good. If he had finished his degree years prior, he would have never taken a class that led us to our counselor (his previous teacher) who we see now. A counselor who has poured so much into us and brought us to a new place of marital healing with so much hope for the future and no room for talk of divorce. I finally feel refreshed in our counseling because it is strictly biblical in nature. It is exactly what we need, and it is Spirit-led. I thank the Lord for how this all shook out. Now, when seeds of doubt pop into my mind surrounding hard situations, I have this tangible reminder that the Lord's plans are perfect. It is a reminder to me that in my sickness, I can trust the Lord's timing and perfect will, which I may not see yet but can lean into with hope for how He will use it.

So, after a week in Ghana together, Spencer flew home with Liam on April 5th. In the meantime, we were still waiting for the birth certificate to be processed. At that point, it had been a month in the making, with no end in sight. I did everything I could to try to get that document. I spent days sitting in Jeffrey's car outside the births and deaths office, drenched in sweat, simply praying to see the right person who could get the work done for us. To be honest, I don't know what finally worked in getting the job done, as I approached it from several angles. My determination was as strong as the journey was hard. We received that birth certificate on April 22, 2024, nearly six weeks after applying for it.

In the waiting, the Lord really did a work in my heart and blessed me along the way. After Liam had left, I got to spend a lot of time with Bismark. It was just the two of us riding it out until the end. He was in school five days a week at that point, so I also had a lot of alone time. That time was precious and healing to my soul. Had I never known what it was like to be physically alone and separated from everyone, I would have never known what it was like to fully lean on the Lord daily. He was all I had. I was able to really focus on my walk with the Lord and grow in knowledge of Him. I spent time doing my own Bible studies, reading scripture, and hanging out with godly friends I had met. In fact, one friend was so gracious as to allow Bismark and me to live in her house with her and her family during our last few weeks in Ghana. I spent time with Bismark eating Peanut Butter M&Ms (my favorite, which I learned I would forever have to share as he loved them as much as me), watching Paw Patrol, getting breakfast out, and going to different locations to play. The time we had together was beautiful in how I was able to view adoption during this "down" season of simply being present.

The realities of adoption are difficult. I have heard people say, "I would never adopt because I have seen how hard it is on the families who choose to adopt." I understand the sentiment behind this and not wanting to make life harder, but life isn't about being as comfortable as possible. In fact, I have come to learn that growth and sanctification happen most through the hard things we face. We chose to step into "hard" when we chose to adopt, but we did so knowing that that was where the Lord called us to and that He would make a way for us. We have already seen so much beauty come out of the difficulty of adoption and how it has also shaped our children. I pray that by us choosing something hard that displays the gospel will be something that the children will always lean into. I pray that when faced with hard decisions in the future, our children choose the route that glorifies the Lord, even if it is the more difficult option. I have another journal entry that I would love to share with you so you can see where my heart has been and the areas in which my heart has grown.

April 13, 2024

"This afternoon, I took Bismark to an indoor play place. He and I both loved it. It was such a fun space to play in for a very low price. As he played, I read. As I read, I prayed. As I prayed, I contemplated all that God had done and was doing. I don't know how many of you know this, but the reason we said yes to adoption from Ghana was because of all the African nations, it required the shortest time in the country. Initially, we were only expected to be in Ghana for one month. One month felt like a comfortable time frame for us financially and logistically.

Now, I both laugh and confess my heart to the Lord. I laugh because the joke's on us—I have been here for almost five months. I confess because I shouldn't obey God solely based on my comfort. Thankfully, the Lord still used our comfortable obedience and our hearts' motives. If we had known at the time of signing a contract with an agency that being in Ghana was going to be roughly four months (let alone five and counting), we probably wouldn't have signed it at all. Which means we would not know and love our Bismark. It breaks my heart to know that my fear of being uncomfortable and not trusting God's plan could have kept me from the beautiful gift that is Bismark. As I sat at that play place, I sat in awe of who Bismark is. I was not able to have what many would deem meaningful conversations with Bismark yet due to language, trust, and developmental barriers, so I would admire him in silence many times as he ate.

I have always wanted our adoption journey to be real and God-honoring. Part of that would involve sharing our journey honestly. Within the first couple weeks of having Bismark in our care, someone said, "It's like he's always been a part of the family." Honestly, my shame inside was screaming, "What? This kid has completely disrupted our lives. I definitely don't feel like he has always been a part of the family... and wonder if I ever will." I never

166

shared that out loud because shame kept me from expressing my heart. I was wrestling inside as if I should feel guilty for feeling that way. I have also struggled with feelings of "what have I done to our lives? Life will never look the same. Have I done a disservice to our biological children?"

You know what? Our lives WILL never look the same. My prayer is that it looks more like Jesus and points to Him. It looks more like love. It looks more like grace. It looks more like mercy. And it looks a little bit messier. And as for our biological children, they love Bismark! They will hardly remember a life without him. Liam and Bismark are growing up like twins and they love each other dearly. It is so fun to watch them interact and play together. Bismark enriches all of our lives.

Over time, I was able to view my feelings from a healthier perspective. I even wrote down my thoughts as I felt the tides shifting. 'Although we still have hard days and difficult moments, I am feeling

167

the love for Bismark more like the love I have for my biological children.'

Everyone talks about the attachment issues an orphaned child may have with adoptive parents and other adults, but no one talks about the attachment issues an adoptive parent may have with an adopted child. Knowing that instinctive, burning motherly love of bearing a child made me feel less than when I didn't have that feeling in the beginning for Bismark. The first days with Bismark felt very honeymoon-like as we enjoyed watching who he was. However, I learned quickly that love was an action. Of course, I know this, but having to face love as an action without a feeling every day was very humbling to me. I have an entry from another day that read, 'Now as I love in action by meeting basic needs, the *feeling* of love and attachment are forming. I have always loved Bismark, but I am thankful that the feeling of love is continually growing.'

The complexity and beauty of adoption are not lost on me. One of my favorite quotes, by Jody Landers says, "A child born to another woman calls me mommy. The magnitude of that tragedy and the depth of that privilege are not lost on me.'" (End Journal Entry)

I had a lot of time to reflect on my heart as Bismark's mom, as well as lean into an adoption counselor while overseas. There is a really interesting dynamic of raising a five-year-old who is more developmentally like a three-year-old, yet has tendencies in certain areas of a nearly ten-year-old. Bismark knows how to manipulate and fight for what he wants. He had to. He lived for nearly five years, competing and trying to survive; learning how to parent that is difficult. Also, while Liam will always be the youngest in age amongst our children, Bismark initially was functionally the youngest. Being the "baby" was functionally ripped away from Liam in a unique way. Bismark has a traumatic past and a story that I will never know and he may never be able to express. I have struggled with the question, "Lord, are you sure I am equipped to raise Bismark?" And you know what the still voice said to me? "No, you aren't. But I am." Likewise, outside of Christ, I am unable to raise my biological children in a God-honoring way.

After receiving that birth certificate on April 22, I wish that I could say the rest of the process went smoothly. We immediately applied for Bismark's passport so that we could make his medical appointment to receive his visa. The passport went smoothly and quickly. Our agency informed us that things should be pretty smooth sailing moving forward as we would no longer have to rely on Ghanaian systems to finish up our process. We attended Bismark's medical appointment the same day we received his passport so as not to waste any time. We were so close to the finish line, and I was sprinting. The appointment went well…until it didn't. We knew that it would take a few days for the embassy to receive Bismark's medical information but that we could schedule his visa appointment while waiting. So, we did. A few days later, we woke up excited for the appointment, knowing that we would be able to fly home a few days later, just in time for Mother's Day.

The morning of the visa appointment, I received a phone call that changed everything. The medical team needed to see us back at the office. I instantly knew that something was majorly wrong. No other family had reported anything of this nature, and my heart sank. I dropped everything I was doing and headed back to the office to clarify the situation. I sat in front of the doctor, weeping and pleading as she informed me that we would have to put Bismark through more medical testing before we could be granted our visa, and that could mean being in Ghana for possibly another eight weeks. She informed me that there was nothing she could do to change that decision. With that in mind, I still showed up that afternoon at our scheduled visa appointment. The consular officer also informed me that until she had the go-ahead from the medical team, she could not grant Bismark his visa.

That day broke me. The pit in my stomach and the heartache I felt throughout my body were indescribable. I allowed myself to weep all day while being comforted by friends and still planning how to proceed. Truthfully, I was broken, but I had to keep fighting. In the midst of all of the chaos, Spencer and I were faced with another crossroads. We had to decide what would be best for me and for the entire family. Spencer was drowning back home, transporting children to stay at different places on different nights of the week, homeschooling the kids, finishing his schooling, and working full time. Meanwhile, I was drowning in the weariness of the adoption process while also desperately missing the other kids. With the new realizations and uncertainty of timing, we decided that it would be best for everyone if I returned home until they informed us that we could pick up Bismark's visa.

The days leading up to my departure were difficult as I dealt with the weight of leaving Bismark with a foster parent in my absence. Thankfully,

Asana stepped up to the plate and happily agreed to take care of him on our behalf. I also dealt with the agonizing effects of forcing Bismark to undergo traumatic medical testing, which I mourned the entire flight back home. The other major piece I had to come to terms with was the loss of a dream. I am a dreamer by nature. Since starting the adoption process, I had a dream of a homecoming reception with an airport full of people excitedly welcoming us home and meeting Bismark. That dream grew bigger as our time in Ghana took longer. Instead, I knew that I would be going home with no son in my arms and no large reception.

Prior to going home, I tried to prepare Bismark's heart for my absence. I informed him that I would be going to the "big yellow house" and reassured him I would be back for him soon. I also told him that I needed to go to the "big yellow house" in order to pick up a remote-controlled fire truck he had seen and really wanted. I also learned a valuable lesson through the hardship of leaving. Not only did I have to leave Bismark, but I had to force him to undergo medical testing before I left. He was suffering at the doing of my hands as I physically held him down for the testing. However, I did it for his good. I did it so that he could eventually come to the "big yellow house." He couldn't see that or even understand it when I explained it to him. But that was the truth. I am learning that sometimes, the Lord may allow us to go through challenging experiences for our own good. I can choose to go through difficult things kicking, fighting, and resisting, just like Bismark did, knowing it will only make it harder. Or, I can choose to trust that what I go through will result in what the Lord deems best for my life, as He brings the "good" on the other side of the hard.

Challenge/Question for Thought: What hard situation are you resisting that you could allow God to use for your good and His glory? Do you have examples in your life to which you can refer and see how God worked things together in ways that only He could do—to bring about a better plan? How can you use those examples to help you through current hard situations?

CHAPTER 13

Great Blessing

By God's grace, my trip home to refresh and keep me strong for the rest of the journey was only a little over one week. The documents we needed in order to receive Bismark's visa took about two weeks in total. So, I hopped back on a plane to Ghana after spending some time at home. I spent three days back in the country, which was a whirlwind from jet lag, saying my goodbyes and finishing up some final errands. On May 18, 2024, Bismark and I hopped on a plane to America. We arrived home to a beautiful crowd of our closest family members. While it may not have happened exactly the way I always dreamed of, the sight will forever be etched in my mind and one I wish I had recorded from my perspective. To see the people I love the most holding up signs and balloons to welcome us home was truly a blessing.

I have drawn so much encouragement from the story of Joseph in Genesis. Many of you probably know the story, but I will recap it here for you. Joseph had many brothers, but he was his father's favorite. His father made him an ornate robe, and all of his brothers hated him because of the status he held with their father. Joseph began sharing dreams he had of his brothers bowing down to him, which made them all the more hateful. The brothers plotted to kill Joseph one day but, ultimately, decided to spare his life. Instead, they sold him to the Ishmaelites, who sold him to an official in Egypt. The brothers reported back to their father, Jacob, that Joseph had been killed in the fields. Although Joseph was sold off, "The Lord was with Joseph, and he became a successful man, and he was in the house of his Egyptian master" (Genesis 39:2). Joseph became the overseer of the house, and everything was blessed because of him. Later, the master's wife wanted to lie with Joseph, but he refused. She then crafted a plan and lied to the master by saying that Joseph tried to lie with her but fled when she cried out. Her sinful deceit led him to prison, even when he continued to live a life of integrity. It would seem as if the enemy had won, "But the Lord was with Joseph and showed him steadfast love and gave him favor in the sight of the keeper of the prison." (Genesis. 39:21)

Eventually, a cupbearer to the king and a baker were placed in prison under Joseph's care. Joseph interpreted dreams for the two individuals that came to fruition at a later time. Two years later, Pharoah had a dream that no one could interpret, and the cupbearer recalled Joseph's ability to interpret dreams. Pharoah called for Joseph to interpret his dream. Joseph did so, giving credit to God as the provider of the interpretation. Pharoah was pleased and put Joseph in charge of all the land of Egypt at the age of thirty. Having known that a famine would enter the land, Joseph spent seven years storing up grain in preparation and then selling it to all of Egypt when the famine hit. Joseph's brothers were among the people seeking to buy food. Joseph recognized them, but they did not recognize him. Joseph made a deal with them to bring back their youngest brother, Benjamin, while he kept another brother, Simeon, captive. The brothers later returned with Benjamin when they needed more food. Upon their return, they enjoyed a meal together with Joseph. Through a series of events, Joseph revealed himself to his brothers. In Genesis 45:8, Joseph says, "So it was not you who sent me here, but God..." Joseph then blessed his family and brought them all to Egypt and was reunited with his father. Once Jacob died, the brothers feared any possible grudge that Joseph may have against them. They offered themselves as slaves to Joseph, and then Joseph says one of the most profound things that holds so much significance. In Genesis 50:20, we read, "As for you, you meant evil against me, but God meant it for good, to bring it about that many people should be kept alive, as they are today."

If Joseph's brothers had never sold him, he would have never gone to prison. Had he never gone to prison, he would have never met the cupbearer. Had he never met the cupbearer, he would have never had the opportunity to interpret the king's dream. Had he never interpreted the dream, he never would have risen to power. Had he never risen to power, he would have never been able to store up food to curb the effects of famine. Had he never stored up food, many people, including his brothers, would have died. Joseph went through years of hardship, being sold by his brothers, falsely accused by his master's wife, and spending time in prison. But God. He used every single circumstance to work together for the saving of thousands of lives. It took years for Joseph to realize the plan that was intended for his life—years of both the good and the bad.

Much like the evil that the brothers intended against Joseph, the Enemy tried to keep my family from experiencing the fullness of the blessing that the Lord had prepared for us. He tried to thwart the Lord's plan, but we are so thankful for God's faithfulness to bring us through many years of both hardship and growth. While I may not have yet arrived at physical healing, I trust that the Lord will continue to use my health to deepen my roots in Him. If I have to go through more years of challenging circumstances, I will choose to look to Joseph's story as an encouragement to my heart. What the Enemy has planned (and is planning) to use for evil against me, the Lord has used (and will continue to use) it for good.

My only desire for this entire book has been for Christ to be glorified… nothing more, nothing less. I pray that my vulnerability can be an encouragement to anyone going through difficult circumstances and that I can share the hope that I have in Jesus. In fact, just like I have had to borrow hope from others in my medical journey, I pray that you can borrow hope from me in whatever situation you find yourself. But most importantly, I pray that you borrow hope from the God who gives us hope when all else seems lost. We are not hopeless because of who we serve, but sometimes, we need reminders while in the trenches. God cares personally about my journey the same way He cares personally about YOUR journey. Jesus Himself can also relate to our suffering. In Luke 22:42, Jesus pleads to the Father, "Saying, 'Father if you are willing, remove this cup from me. Nevertheless, not my will, but yours, be done.'" Jesus was in agony as He cried out to the Father to take away His suffering and the death that was soon to come. We serve a God who allowed His only son to suffer and be killed for our good. Now that is a hope we can draw upon.

Choosing to stop the adoption process due to my health condition would not necessarily have been a sinful decision for Spencer and me to make. While there would have been legitimacy in that decision, I am thankful for the passion and tenacity that the Lord placed in my heart, followed by His supernatural power bringing us through. If we chose not to continue to adopt, we would have missed out on the entirety of the blessing God had for us. Would we have learned a lot regardless? Absolutely. Could God have still used us in other

181

ways for the Kingdom? Without a doubt. Would we have grown as a family in different ways by surrendering our plans? Of course. *But*, would we have our Bismark? No.

We wouldn't have the little boy who called me "Ma" only a few short days after meeting me. We wouldn't have the boy who lights up our lives with so much joy and laughter. We wouldn't have two little boys who have the dearest brotherly relationship I have ever seen. We wouldn't have the joy of watching Bismark experience all new and exciting things. We wouldn't have witnessed miracles in Ghana. We wouldn't have been humbled by experiencing another culture and allowing the beauty of how others do life to impact our hearts. We wouldn't have the personal experience and understanding of the link between earthly and heavenly adoption. We would have missed life-changing moments of trusting in the Lord and watching His faithfulness in our lives. We would have missed the lessons that we have learned as a result of dependency on the Lord. We would have missed witnessing the miraculous timing of the Lord, allowing us to grow in our knowledge of who He is. We would simply have missed out on so much.

In regard to the adoption, I feel our story resonates with that of Joseph. We went through a lot of difficulty, but we have now arrived at the blessing. While we still have a life of learning as we raise Bismark, the logistics and legalities surrounding adoption have come to an end. On the contrary, my medical journey still often feels like I am in prison, much like that from where Paul rejoiced. I have not arrived at the end by seeing my physical body restored. I pray I do arrive at healing on this side of Heaven, but if not, I will make it my life's aim to honor and glorify the One who created me regardless of my physical state.

In Philippians 3:12, Paul writes from prison, "Not that I have already obtained this or am already perfect, but I press on to make it my own, because Christ Jesus has made me his own." I want to echo

Paul's words because he expresses my thoughts perfectly. Throughout the entirety of this book, I have wrestled with sharing all I have learned throughout my journey because it has taken me four years to come to a place in which I can look back and see the lessons. In the same breath, I believe that my story is really God's story, so I want to share it to spur others on in the faith obediently. I have gone through four incredibly hard years, and my perspective has taken years to shift. I absolutely have not handled things well more times than I can count. The growth that has happened (and is still happening) in my life came as a result of my situations, not that I had it all figured out while going through my situations. They say hindsight is 20/20, and that is so true. As I have witnessed God's faithfulness over the past four years, I pray that I will always look back on these years and remember them. I want to remember, as Brandon Lake's "Adoption Song" states, that when the Liar starts mouthing off, I can sing in confidence, MY adoption song.

Challenge/Question for Thought: I will circle back around to the question I posed at the beginning of this book. What passion has the Lord placed on your heart? How can you lean into obedience and allow God to use that passion for your good and His glory? How can you keep your focus on Christ so that you can persevere even when things get rocky?

Epilogue

I wanted to share a quick update about how Bismark has transitioned back home to the States. Upon arriving home, Bismark has slept in his bed since day one. He has gone to bed and stayed in bed without any issues. We believe that this is one of the benefits of being in Ghana for so long. We had time to build trust with Bismark and allow him to be comfortable in our care. We spent time in Ghana showing Bismark pictures of his Spiderman bed back home, in the same room as Liam. He has surpassed all expectations, as we were warned that coming back home would be like starting all over again. The Lord has totally blessed us in this regard.

Bismark has since been engaged on a soccer team and a basketball team. He is enrolled in a hybrid school that allows him to have formal instruction while also experiencing a homeschool education. He loves to play more than anything else. He will build with tiles for hours on end as he is very hands-on. He also loves riding his bike and going to playgrounds. Bismark has a belly laugh that we all love to hear, and he enjoys skipping and dancing with joy throughout the house. He is anxiously waiting for snow to fall and talks about his first birthday party here with great anticipation. He has a heart of service and obeys so well. He has jumped right into our church's children's program and Awana with no hesitation. His relationship with Liam is full of both fun and competition. They are the best of friends but also fight like brothers. Bismark is truly flourishing. Of course, we have challenges, but we wanted to reflect the goodness of God all over his life and ours.

We are privileged to raise Bismark alongside our other three children. We have seen the beauty of having biological children prior to bringing Bismark into our lives. The four of them have truly helped each other in the transition without ever speaking of it out loud. Our days are full of great fondness and utter chaos, and we wouldn't have it any other way. Thank you for joining us on our journey and allowing us to share Jesus in all of it!

"Now to him who is able to do far more abundantly than all that we ask or think, according to the power at work within us, to him be glory in the church and in Christ Jesus throughout all generations, forever and ever. Amen."

Ephesians 3:20-21

Studies have found that there are 140-153 million orphaned children worldwide.

All profits from the sale of this book will be donated to help fight the orphan crisis.

December 12, 2023. Ashton, Bismark, and Spencer shortly after meeting for the first time.

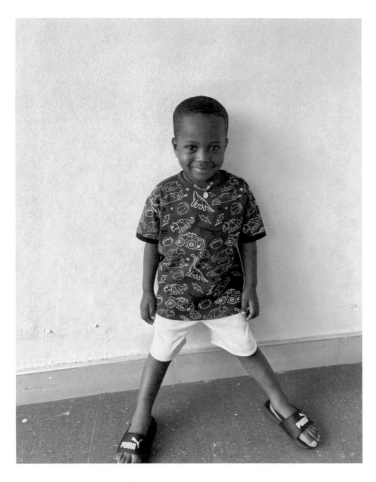

December 13, 2023. Bismark in his new clothes the day
we brought him from the orphanage.

December 20, 2023. On our safari at Mole National Park in Tamale, Ghana. Liam, Zyan, Bismark, and Nyla.

December 25, 2023. Our first Christmas with Bismark.
Nyla, Zyan, Liam, and Bismark.

January 1, 2024. Bismark's 5th birthday.

January 28, 2024. Family picture taken before
Spencer left to share once we finalized the adoption in court.

February 17, 2024. The kiddos in their matching
Ghanaian apparel.

February 27, 2024. Court Day. The day that Bismark
legally became our son!

March 31, 2024. Easter. The boys being silly before heading to an Easter get-together with friends.

May 15, 2024. The day that we were able to pick up
Bismark's visa to the United States.

May 18, 2024. Ashton and Bismark at the airport starting
the journey to America.

May 18, 2024. Bismark being greeted by
his siblings awaiting his arrival.

May 18, 2024. Family waiting at the airport to greet
Ashton and Bismark upon their arrival in the states.

July 4, 2024. Bismark celebrating his first American Independence
Day.

October 18, 2024. Bismark celebrating his first Halloween as
Marshall from his favorite show, Paw Patrol.

October 2024. Fall family picture.

October 2024. Bismark fall photograph.

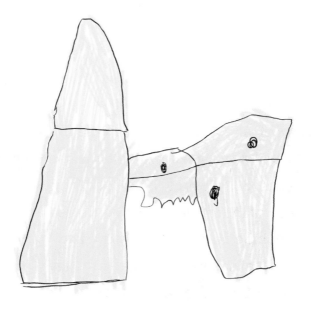

Bismark's drawing of the "Big Yellow House".

About the Author

Ashton is an incredible mother, wife, friend, teacher, interpreter, and now author. Interweaving throughout all of these roles that she holds, she prioritizes the relationship that is most important to her: Jesus. She desires to do everything well, with His seal of approval being her most influential guide. Ashton has a huge heart and harnesses these big feelings to serve God, her family, and her community. She absolutely adores her children and has soaked up every stage of their upbringing thus far. While Ashton strives to put Jesus first in everything she does, she does have some fun hobbies that make her who she is. She loves playing cards with her parents and grandparents and board games with her brothers' families on the weekends. She has a weakness for the show Friends and enjoys watching movies and football with others. With all of this said, she is a beautiful soul who hopes that through this book, the readers can feel the tension between being blessed, being challenged, and being equipped to love God and love people.

About the book

Upon getting married and starting a biological family, Ashton and her husband began their international adoption journey.

"Big Yellow House" takes you on a personal journey of Ashton's growth, marital healing, and a six-month trip to Ghana.

If you are experiencing challenges, struggling to persevere, losing hope in a situation, or simply want to feel encouraged to keep fighting the good fight for the Lord, this book is for you. In light of all of this, please join the multi-faceted, physical and spiritual journey of chronic illness, marriage, and international adoption.

*TMM*PUBLISHING

Here are a few highlights about TMM Publishing

1) We don't take out any royalties

2) You keep your intellectual property (You own your book)

3) You don't have to have a manuscript to start; you only have to have an idea. (We help you develop it)

4) You can purchase your book at wholesale price (no third party or up-charging)

5) Not only are we going to develop and publish your book, but we will help you successfully launch your book.

Are you called to write and publish? It's time to be faithful to the call.

213

Visit our website at www.TMMPublishing.com and book a Free 30-minute consultation. Or text " book" to (321) 471 1944

Made in the USA
Columbia, SC
09 February 2025

53529525R00124